The Closet Entrepreneur

337 Ways to Start Your Successful Business With Little or No Money

By Neil Balter

With Carrie Shook

Career Press
180 Fifth Avenue
P.O. Box 34
Hawthorne, NJ   07507
1-800-CAREER-1
201-427-0229 (Outside U.S.)
FAX: 201-427-2037

THE CLOSET ENTREPRENEUR

ISBN 1-56414-138-1, $14.95

Cover design by A Good Thing, Inc.

Printed in the U.S.A. by Book-mart Press

To order this title by mail, please include price as noted above, $2.50 handling per order, and $1.00 for each book ordered. Send to: Career Press, Inc., 180 Fifth Ave., P.O. Box 34, Hawthorne, NJ 07507.

Or call toll-free 1-800-CAREER-1 (Canada: 201-427-0229) to order using VISA or MasterCard, or for further information on books from Career Press.

Library of Congress Cataloging-in-Publication Data

Balter, Neil, 1960-
    The closet entrepreneur : more than 50 ways to start your successful business with little or no money / by Neil Balter with Carrie Shook.
      p. cm.
    Includes index.
    ISBN 1-56414-138-1 $14.95
    1. New business enterprises--Management. 2. Success in business.
I. Shook, Carrie. II. Title.
HD62.5.B355   1994
658'.1'11--dc20
                                        94-3750
                                         CIP

DEDICATION

This book is dedicated to my parents, Jack and Roberta, and my brother Craig. Without their support, my dreams would never have come true.

Neil

ACKNOWLEDGEMENTS

The authors are grateful to many people who made valuable contributions in the preparation of this book: Rubens Apovian, Mark Arnold, Richard Bloch, Peter Bustetter, Frank Carney, Bill Cherkasky, Burt Cohen, Fred DeLuca, Jo-Anne Dressendorfer, Rob Dunn, Mohamed Fathelbab, Marvin Feuerman, Steve Feuerman, Errol Frankel, Bob Hutchinson, Verne Harnish, Steven Krane, Howard Lester, Bill LeVine, Doug Mellinger, Jeff Meyer, Jon Meyer, Rauer Meyer, Lisa Morris, Reg Pattemore, Arnold Price, Steve Reuning, Buck Rogers, Bill Rosenberg, Elinor Shook, Michael Shook, R.J. Shook, Robert L. Shook, David Seigel, Jack Stack, Zack Suchman, Peter Thomas, Jim Trethewey, Bill Trimble, Anthony Vidergauz, Michael K.L. Wager, Richard Weiner, and all the other countless people that helped us along the way.

Finally, we thank our friends in the publishing aspect of our endeavor. Jeff Herman, our agent and good friend, whom we think is the best in his field; we deeply appreciate his belief in our writing projects. And it was our good fortune to work with exceptional people at Career Press—our editor Betsy Sheldon, Ellen Scher, production manager, and Ron Fry, our publisher.

When writers are blessed with so many supporters and friends, the task of writing a book is indeed a pleasurable one.

CONTENTS

INTRODUCTION

At age 17, I was as improbable a candidate to start my own business as there ever was. Not only did I have zero experience, I had struggled just to make it through high school. But, in retrospect, I did have a few things going for me. I had desire, enormous energy and I was too naive to know how much the odds were stacked against me.

In 1978, my involvement in the business world began purely by accident. I moved out of my parents house when I was a senior in high school because of irreconcilable differences. I was staying out all hours of the night and my grades were terrible. I had caused my parents and teachers a lot of grief.

So, there I was out on my own. Now I had to pull my act together and find a way to support myself. And thus began the California Closet Company.

My small company eventually grew into an international business with nearly 100 franchises, with locations in the United States, Australia, Canada, Japan, New Zealand and Spain. In 1989, gross sales hit $70 million, and one year later the company was acquired by Williams-Sonoma, Inc.

For the first time since I was 17, I am no longer in the closet business. Having founded a company, operated it and sold it, I've completed the full cycle. I am getting myself geared to start a new venture.

Before I do, however, I've decided it's time to fulfill another ambition—to write this book—based on my experiences and thoughts as an entrepreneur. I became convinced of the need for this book through my involvement with Young Entrepreneur's Organization, an association of young business owners, of which I was a founding member and past president. At YEO functions, I became acquainted with dozens of other young entrepreneurs, each with their own fascinating success story, few of whom discovered great wisdom from the conventional business books available at the time.

After sharing and learning from so many other business owners' experiences, I discovered a need for a practical book about how to start a business written by a person who really knows. Personally, while I was learning the ropes, I had difficulty buying into the so-called how-to-start-a-new-business books—they were so theoretical, written by authors who never operated their own businesses. Based on my own experience, I figure the entrepreneurs running their own successful businesses were too busy to write books. Now between businesses, I enjoy the unusual opportunity of taking a breather to write such a book.

Most importantly, I believe there is a need for this book. Of course, writing a book to fill a need in the marketplace is not unlike what a successful entrepreneur does. It is not enough to go into a business simply because that's what you want to do. There must be a need for being in it. If not, you are apt to come up with another Edsel.

Today, people ask me: "Did you ever think California Closets would become the company it is today?"

My stock answer is: "Not in my wildest dreams."

Nor did I imagine I'd ever write a book about entrepreneuring. Still, if I did not believe I had a valuable message to tell, I wouldn't want my name on a book. My goal is for this book to serve as a guide for the millions of Americans who want to start their own business. They'll undoubtedly make mistakes along the way—just like I did. Some could suffer serious financial setbacks, even go belly-up. Hopefully, these pages will steer them in the right direction.

I figure if a guy like me could do what I did, there must be a lot of people who could succeed beyond their wildest dreams, too. Perhaps you're one of those dreamers. My goal for this book is to help you see your hopes and dreams come true.

CHAPTER 1

Starting with a Concept

Few entrepreneurs would dispute the role a mind-boggling idea plays in getting a company off the ground. There are, however, only a few such revolutionary breakthroughs during the span of a single generation—ones such as 3M's ubiquitous Post-it Notes or the computer chip. Then there are hundreds of thousands of great ideas that go by the wayside each year because nobody acts on them. Lest we forget, every business venture begins with an idea.

Paul Hawken, co-founder and chief executive officer of the $70 million direct-marketing firm Smith & Hawken, says, "However it is going to turn out, the seeds are in the beginning." He believes you can't start a good business with a bad concept. If you don't have a good concept or a needed product, you won't have a long-term success. You will know if your concept is a good one when you ask your customers what they think of your product. This is why it is imperative to do as much market research as you can afford (this can be done relatively inexpensively). More importantly, you must really enjoy and be excited about your concept.

While I agree you must have a burning desire, a willingness to work day and night, seven days a week, for several years until your company has been firmly established, there must also be a demand for your products and/or services. Make sure your concept is one that fulfills a void in the marketplace. If it does not, find one that does!

1

Having a good concept

Just how important is it to start with a good concept? In my estimation, it is essential. Beginning a new business with a weak concept is difficult. No matter how hard you work at it, if its basic premise is poor, odds are you'll fail.

I recommend that as a would-be entrepreneur, you do your homework in advance before starting a new business. Find out if there is a need for what you offer to the public. Too often, people start a company simply because it is a business they want to be in. Perhaps they're tired of working for someone else or they don't like the business they already own. Just wanting to be in a particular business is not good enough. The graveyard is filled with small companies that were doomed from their inception.

Did you ever go to a movie where you liked everything about it—the acting, the scenery, the musical background, the special effects—but the story itself was horrendous? It doesn't matter what else the movie has going for it, without a good screenplay, it can never be a good motion picture. Like a movie with a poor script, no matter how much time and money you pour into a business, if it starts off with a weak concept, the odds are against its success.

One of the mistakes that people make when they are researching a new concept, is they don't listen to legitimate criticism. They want everyone to tell them their idea is a great one. I realize it's very easy to become caught up in the excitement of starting a new business, but you must pay attention to the advice you are given. If people have the nerve to tell you they see problems with your concept, listen to them and address each issue without haste.

How my concept was born

Although the basic concept of organizing a closet had been around long before me, nobody ever organized closets as a profession. Most people just hired a carpenter to build shelves. My involvement in the business began purely by accident when I was 17 years old.

It was then, as a senior in high school, that I moved out of my parents' house because of irreconcilable differences. I was staying out all hours of the night and my grades were terrible. I had caused my parents and teachers a lot of grief. So there I was out on my own. I had to pull my act together and find a way to support myself.

One day after school, I was at my best friend Steve Feuerman's house. His father, Marvin, knew I had carpentry skills, and asked me if I would build some shelves in his cramped closet. I needed extra money, so I agreed to do the project. Before I started, we sat down, and looked through a few *Sunset* magazines for ideas. The next day, I bought lumber and other materials, and began remodeling the closet. Marvin was so pleased with my work that he invited his neighbors over to see the improved closet. They were so impressed, they hired me to do the same for them.

Marvin and I thought organizing closets was such a great idea, he convinced me to start my own business doing it. Owning my own business and having a career specializing in closet organization sounded great to me, but everybody I talked to thought I was crazy.

I had no capital to start such a venture. You can imagine my surprise when Marvin offered to help me start my business—with a concept no one had previously done. In exchange for a piece of my company, he gave me $1,000, a van, and helped me file for a license. He also helped me hire an artist for my first advertising—fliers I placed on car windshields.

Most people I met—including accountants, attorneys and business managers told me I wouldn't make it. "No one has done this before!" "You have no education or capital!" Or "How do you think you are going to make this work?" At the same time, nobody ever said it was a stupid idea, which gave me the confidence I needed to know I was onto something good. Even people who couldn't afford to have their closets remodeled or didn't want to, thought it was a good idea.

After two years of partnership, Marvin decided it was time to pursue other business interests. In the meantime, my parents and I reconciled our differences and after a brief stint of retirement, my father was ready to re-enter the business world. The timing couldn't have been better—Marvin wanted to sell his interests so my father and I bought him out for $20,000.

The basic concept behind California Closets was organization—I did not really sell a product. I told my customers, "For $500, I'll take your messy closet and make it nice and organized. You'll be able to find your shoes and sweaters and you will have more hanging space." An important part of my concept was that I didn't want to be involved in a job that required more than one day to complete. This is why I never offered custom-made materials to my customers and never went into remodeling kitchens. I did expand into garage organizing, which was not unlike what I was doing with closets.

Once you decide to pursue a business that offers a product or a service, I recommend you immediately find some potential customers and ask them if they would use it. Is your product something they would spend money on? And how much would they be willing to spend for it? Entrepreneurs sometimes develop a product and then try to sell it. They should have gone to the customer first and then designed a product that has a price point to meet their needs. I did get into some trouble when my company manufactured a garage organization unit that was too expensive for my customer base. I neglected to first ask people how much they would be willing to spend to organize their garages. I acted like I was the know-it-all and told my customers what they needed and how much. Ready, fire, aim. I learned my lesson.

Strange as it seems, it was a disadvantage that my company had no competition. At times I felt I was just stumbling around aimlessly. I had to learn from my own mistakes—not those of others. Fortunately, I had a good basic concept, and I listened to my customers, so my mistakes didn't threaten the survival of the business.

How Celestial Seasonings Inc. started

Mo Siegel, was barely 21 and almost flat broke when he started an herbal tea company called Celestial Seasonings Inc. A travel lover whose hobby was the study of herbs and their medicinal uses, Siegel trekked around Europe to collect information about tea consumption. "I was so interested in herbs," he says, "I spent all my time working on them, studying them, and thinking about them."

Then he tested his flavored brews by serving them to customers in the health-food store he owned in Aspen, Colorado. Since herbal products were sold almost entirely for health purposes, the general public did not see herb teas as something to drink for enjoyment. Although herbal teas were a staple of the European diet, and several U.S. manufacturers had been in the business for as long as 50 years, "Nobody was doing a decent job of it," Siegel said.

For Siegel, "doing a decent job" meant creating teas so good that people would buy them for the taste. "I thought how great it would be if I could make the herb tea taste so good that people would drink it, and then they'd get the health benefits," the entrepreneur said. Study and experimentation led Siegel to combinations of herbs. "I wouldn't have just plain peppermint," he explained. "I'd stick in some chamomile, or a bit of hibiscus, or something else. At that time, nobody sold blends in this country except for medicinal purposes."

The pioneer in the herbal tea industry was careful not to sink everything he had into his products until he tested them on his health-food store customers. "A person who goes out there and blindly attempts something makes a mistake," warned Siegel, whose company's 1993 gross sales totaled over $59 million. "The world is sophisticated, tough, and ruthless. If I had a passion for a cup of tea that only I was going to like, I should have made just one tea bag."

Siegel went ahead with his concept though others discouraged him. "Once I do my homework and my confidence level is high, I don't care what others say," Siegel said matter-of-factly. "Sure, I may fail. I've failed plenty of times. But I guess the key is how willing you are to stick with an idea and hammer away at it. No matter how grim things get, you've got to be persistent. When we first started this company I was poor, but I knew it had to succeed if I just kept working. I had a vision, and it just had to come to be."

REMEMBER

1. If you don't have a good concept or a needed product, no matter how hard you work, you won't have a long-term business.
2. Your concept should be one that fulfills a void in the marketplace.
3. You must really enjoy and be excited about your concept.
4. A good concept is new and unique while also providing value and filling a need for the customer.
5. Listen to legitimate criticism and concerns before you move ahead with your concept.
6. Do your homework!

CHAPTER 2

Reinventing the Wheel

People complain to me all the time about how difficult it is to start a business because everything has been done before—all the great ideas have been used. But all is not lost if you haven't found something new and unique—you don't need a new idea to start a company! There are countless business opportunities lurking around every corner, each waiting for a creative mind to bring it to life. These ideas are available for entrepreneurs to discover during everyday life. Great concepts such as Liquid Paper corrective fluid and the microwave were discovered while their inventors were at work, walking down the street, on a vacation or just reading the newspaper. Even seemingly insignificant occurrences such as tying your shoes can lead you to an idea that may bring you great success.

Even though Liquid Paper and the microwave were breakthrough discoveries, successful business ideas do not have to be original. You don't need to reinvent the wheel when you can just improve the wheel. Products that have been around for decades, can often be improved in some way. Many companies have distinguished their products by marketing them differently. Dunkin' Donuts, for example, chose to set up its own storefronts featuring its doughnuts, rather than sell through grocery stores like everyone else. Bill Rosenberg, founder of Dunkin' Donuts, had the vision and drive to find success in a new way no one had yet tried, and did so with products that were not original or hard to find. This entrepreneur flourished even when the odds were against him.

Most concepts can be changed and brought up-to-date. There's a new and better way to do everything. If you choose to use an existing concept, you must discover a different way to do it or improve it. If you just flat-out copy a concept without adding anything to it, you'll have a hard time establishing yourself in the marketplace. Try offering your customers something better than the competition—be it the product, technology, customer service or method of delivery.

Using the competition to your advantage

When starting a business with a concept that has been around for awhile, you are saved the trouble of introducing the public to something new. You can carefully examine your competitors' shortcomings. Mistakes that they have made in the past point out how you can offer something better.

No matter how good an idea is, there is usually a better way to do it. You can improve most anything. People who have been working with the same product day-in and day-out may lose sight of the obvious. It is difficult for them to take a step backwards, to analyze their production, marketing or even customer service. As the saying goes, "they can't see the forest for the trees." Ironically, it is not unusual for someone who knows nothing about a company, to look at it for the first time and say, "How come they don't do it like this?" Often, it could be a great idea.

New market niches in the fast-food industry

McDonald's, the grandfather of the fast-food industry, was first to mass produce restaurants offering hamburgers, fries and shakes. With thousands of franchises and company-owned stores around the world, how could there be room in the marketplace for competition? Yet, Wendy's International acquired a piece of the market by offering the same product with a whole new concept. Rather than cater to families with young children, Wendy's aimed its market at professionals and the more mature customer. Their comfortable seating and custom-ordered hamburgers weren't available under McDonald's mass-produced policy.

Domino's entered a marketplace already dominated by neighborhood pizza parlors and companies such as Pizza Hut and Shakeys. Domino's offered only a new concept—delivery—and did not even have a facility where customers could eat. It limited its market, yet kept the overhead much lower than the competition's. Both Wendy's and Domino's proved it possible to take a proven concept, change it and thereby own a significant piece of the market.

Every business that has been around for years can be copied and improved by someone who may be faster or do it at a lower cost. A small business can change and adapt, while giant companies too often have a lot of fat—overhead and corporate management. While new companies don't have to deal with the same issues as the giants, it is very important for them to identify their market and understand what it really needs.

REMEMBER

7. All is not lost if you have not found something new and unique—you don't need a new idea to start a company!
8. There are countless business opportunities lurking around every corner, each waiting for a creative mind to bring it to life.
9. If you choose an existing concept, find a unique way to do it, just like Wendy's did.
10. Offer your customers something better than the competition—the product, new technology, customer service or method of delivery.
11. Every business that has been around for years can be copied and improved by someone—no matter how good an idea is, there's a better way to do it.

CHAPTER 3

What's in a Name?

One of the most important decisions you make when starting a business is choosing the name for your company. Your company name is a valuable marketing tool that you will undoubtedly spend a lot of time, money and effort promoting. A unique, memorable name stands out in your customers' minds, granting you an edge over your competition. Eventually, this name will become a valuable asset that your company will take great measures to protect.

Your company's name shouldn't be complicated—just one or two syllables your customers can easily remember. Consider the long-term implications of the business name—not just the present but the future. How will your company's name be received in other parts of the country and world when you expand? What will your company's name look like as a logo, on stationery, or reduced or enlarged for advertising spots?

The best company names are unique ones that later became identified with the products they represent. Descriptive names, such as "Clean Car" for a car wash, are not nearly as memorable as unique names. Plus, they are the hardest to get trademarked. Names that are descriptive are vanilla. The more unique the name, the better it is.

Have you ever purchased "Little Shortcake Fingers," "I Scream" or "Bib-Lapel Lithiated Lemon-Lime Soda." You probably are very familiar with each of these products. But, had these products kept their original, descriptive names, they surely would not have survived over the decades. For example, Little Shortcake Fingers are now known as "Twinkies," while I Scream was the original name for "Eskimo Bars." Few remember the time when Bib-Lapel Soda was the brand name for what is now called "7-Up!" Each of these products were originally christened with a clunker of a descriptive name, but saved when given less wordy and more unique brand names.

Of course, no product enjoys immediate recognition without first paying the price. The name Coca-Cola meant nothing to the public until millions of dollars were spent promoting it. Now "Coke" is one of the most recognizable product names in the world. "Kleenex" has become more than a brand name—and has all but replaced the word "tissue" in the English language! Xerox, McDonald's and Kodak are more names that had little to do with the product they represented, yet are now known in every corner of the globe after a great deal of marketing dollars were spent.

Protecting your name

You have to think about the future! New business owners sometimes neglect to investigate their name choice. When business is great and it's time to expand, they are surprised to discover they can't use their name in other states or countries. I recommend hiring an attorney who specializes in trademarks to search nationwide to see if your name has been previously registered. This few hundred dollars is well-worth the cost. After you've spent three or four years advertising your company's name, you don't want to find out that you have to change it down the road because someone else is already using it where you want to expand. Over the years, California Closets became a very recognizable brand name, but only after over $100 million worth of marketing, advertising and promotional work, making it a very valuable asset!

When I first started to expand outside California, I hesitated to use the name *California Closets* because the state of California had a reputation of being a flaky place to live. I was afraid that it would give my company a bad image and customers would not take us seriously. They might think that California Closets would be just another crazy idea from someone in California.

So, instead, I opted for a more descriptive name, *Creative Closets*. My attorney filed the necessary paperwork to register the name Creative Closets, but one week before the trademark was ready to be issued, I received an important letter. An attorney in Allentown, Pennsylvania, wrote that his client, who had been using the Creative Closets name in Pennsylvania, contested my claim. The attorney demanded $20,000 for our right to use the Creative Closets name in his state. We refused to pay.

Fortunately, my attorney secured the right to use the name if we stayed outside of a 100-mile radius around Allentown where the other Creative Closets company was located. We breathed a sigh of relief, but too soon. That same attorney ambitiously sought out four more businesses also using the name Creative Closets in other states, and formed a joint venture between them and the business in Allentown! Now there were Creative Closets in cities such as Washington, D.C., and New York City—barring us from using it there, too.

To make matters worse, the attorney demanded an additional $20,000 for each new business he represented in addition to the one in Allentown. His asking price had gone from $20,000 to $100,000! Rather than be defeated by the new joint venture, I chose to retain California Closets as the name, which I decided sounded fresh and new, and fortunately was not being used anywhere else in the country. This lawsuit actually prevented me from making a serious mistake in using a purely descriptive name.

Protecting your company name in the United States is only half the battle! When your company goes international, you must file trademark applications in every country where you wish to expand. How costly is it? Only $200 to $500 for each country, but it should be done immediately. Believe it or not, there are trademark pirates whose objective is to register your name in foreign countries before you do, forcing you to buy it from them for a high price. Unfortunately, trademark pirates may demand as much as $500,000 to $1 million for the right to use your own company name!

This happened to Burger King when it made plans to open restaurants in Australia. Trademark pirates beat the company in registering the Burger King name, restricting it from using its own name in the entire country! Rather than pay the enormous fee demanded by the pirates, the restaurant opted to use "Home of the Whopper" as its name instead.

ServiceMaster's name

Considered the most profitable service company for the last decade by *Forbes* magazine, with annual sales totaling over $3 billion, ServiceMaster is a one-of-a-kind organization. It provides professional residential and commercial services for cleaning, lawn care, pest control, disaster restoration, maid service, home warranty and appliance repair, and temporary personnel services. The company is set apart from other companies specifically by its principles illustrated by the company's primary corporate objective—"To Honor God in All We Do."

In the 1940s, company founders Marion Wade and Kenneth T. Wessner named their new company Wade, Wessner and Associates, but as the organization grew at a rapid rate, they decided it was too much of a mouthful. The partners thought something more generic would better suit the various functions performed by the company.

According to Wade, "We wanted a name which could be applied to the diversified services we performed and at the same time indicate the basic philosophy of the company. The name we chose evolved almost by itself. As a company, we were in the business of on-location cleaning and maintenance services. As individuals and as a company, we were working for the Lord—we were servants of the master. The word 'ServiceMaster' struck us as perfect in every area." ServiceMaster was an ideal name with its double meaning: *Masters of Service* and *Serving the Master*.

REMEMBER

12. The name should not be complicated—just one or two syllables your customers will remember.
13. The best company names are unique names that later become associated with the products, no doubt giving a competitive edge.
14. Before you settle on a name, hire an attorney specializing in trademark protection to do a nationwide search. Then file the necessary applications to register it.

—

CHAPTER 4

Preparing a Business Plan

Every business needs a detailed business plan. Yes, every business. I know you already have a concept, but that's not enough—you must plan year-to-year. A thorough plan analyzes your business idea from every angle.

A business should include a strategic agenda that you frequently consult while planning your company's future. This projects your company's financial return and anticipates future resource needs. The plan is especially useful during your search for funding—every potential source for capital will ask to see it. People with money to lend or invest attach a great deal of importance to the quality of the plan. They prefer a plan that is thorough and professional and includes details, facts and figures that will help to support your assumptions.

Make it realistic

A good business plan is realistic. It will be helpful to know your weaknesses early and resolve them before they evolve into problems. Your investors will also want to know the potential risks at stake—be upfront and honest with them and you will gain their confidence. The plan should be informative while generating interest and excitement.

Use your business plan to stress your company's strong points, as well as to identify weak points and feasible solutions. Inexperienced business owners may wear rose-colored glasses. Will you reach for pie in the sky or will you have realistic expectations of your young business? Lofty goals can be impossible to meet in the short term. A business plan keeps your company headed in the right direction, and provides you, your management and investors with a broad, realistic perspective of goals.

The plan should be factual, neither too conservative nor too liberal with sales figures. Projected sales, overhead and other expenses for the first year in business must also be realistic. Do not exaggerate sales or profit projections because your investors may think the numbers are too high to be achieved. On the other hand, if your numbers are too nominal, you might not attract any investors.

Projections should be done on a monthly basis for the first year. Include a detailed breakdown of the company's expected income and expenses, accompanied by supporting schedules. The second and third years should be done quarterly and include summaries of the company's anticipated income and expenses.

Avoid setting unattainable goals—instead make them achievable. Don't be too aggressive with your numbers. You won't get shot for being too conservative! If your company doesn't meet goals and investors' expectations, you'll be the villain. It is preferable to be the hero by being a little conservative and surpassing all expectations.

Your company's sales during the first year will probably be lower than you expect. You will spend more money in product development and marketing than you expected, while your gross margins will be thinner and operating costs higher than you thought. Things happen.

Give yourself a fighting chance to get the company off the ground by putting no more pressure on yourself and your employees than absolutely necessary. Your business can have an outstanding first six months, by exceeding rather than not meeting projections.

Simplicity is the key

A simple business plan is the preferable one. It identifies important points about your company while avoiding detail. Such a plan covers important facts, but is not so long that it becomes burdensome to read. The plan should be supplemented by details and background information that may be requested by investors.

A start-up business plan should include the following details:

- ✔ A table of contents.
- ✔ A brief overview describing your company's products or services and the niche you will fill in the marketplace.
- ✔ A statement of purpose: why you believe your business will succeed.
- ✔ A biographical sketch of yourself and each of your key management—this is the first and most important thing an investor will want to review. Emphasize experience in the industry.
- ✔ A summary about your industry, target customer, location of business, projected development schedule, sales and marketing plan, competition and what distinguishes your business from the competition.
- ✔ Strategic issues: long-term goals, corporate philosophy, pricing, distribution, growth strategy, marketing and sales strategies, evolution of product line, development schedule and planned growth.
- ✔ A financial statement and projection of expenses that details your budget, bottom line, fixed assets, cash flow projections, future plans for expansion, start-up costs, equipment costs, hiring schedule and other overhead.
- ✔ Possible exit strategies in which an investor might be able to divest with a profit (public offering, buy-out, etc.)
- ✔ Additional financing sources for credit or capital. List all partners and other investors you may already have. Detail their investment, ownership and control over the business.

Graphics can also help convey the image you want to project. A colorful plan also serves as an example of your marketing skills. Be cautious when using spread sheets and formulas. Take into account many factors that cannot be calculated such as competition, material and labor cost increases, product development and changes in marketing. In reality, your sales will not increase by 5 1/2 percent every month. Some months, your sales will go up 15 percent, and other months, perhaps nothing.

What to plan

A plan should not look forward beyond three years because in today's world, it is too difficult to predict what will happen in the future. Technology and the world change so rapidly—you don't know what the scenario will be in five years. Therefore, create a plan that thoroughly examines the first year and presents the second and third years in a more summarized manner.

Personally, I don't recommend planning ahead further than three years, although others may advise you to plan as far as five to seven years. Large multi-national companies have a much easier time planning this far in advance. The bigger the company, and the more established it is, the longer they plan out. For example, companies such as Procter & Gamble or IBM can plan years in advance, but this isn't realistic for your small or medium-sized company.

This comprehensive business plan should include a budget anticipating bottom line and cash-flow projections in advance. This allows you to manage the business's cash requirements and plan for additional financing required. By planning for downturns and other unanticipated occurrences in advance, you may, one day, avert a short-term cash-flow shortage that could have proven fatal to your company.

A business doesn't always evolve according to plan, so your plan must be flexible. You can't make every decision according to your plan, and there may be factors that arise unexpectedly. Your plan will need to evolve and develop.

Use it or lose it! Don't file your plan away, never to be seen again. A plan should be examined monthly and compared to actual results. This way, you can understand where you went wrong.

Assistance in planning

It is a good idea to use your own management team and/or professional consultants to help you prepare and review your business plan. There are also many software programs you can use that will help organize your plan. Additional assistance can also be found through the following resources: The Small Business Administration, United States Department of Commerce, and various entrepreneurial organizations.

What venture capitalists look for

Bill Trimble, president and CEO of the W.A.T. Capital Corp., a merchant banking and venture capital firm in Vancouver, British Columbia, explains investing in a private company is a great risk. This is why he carefully examines each business plan before considering an investment.

"The very first thing I look at in a business plan is the background of the owner and his or her management—the people," Trimble reveals. "It is very important to consider the people—their knowledge and credibility in the business.

"Then, I evaluate the business's concept or technology," the venture capitalist continues, "Of course, when I spot a wacky concept, there is no need to even look at the company's management. Finally, I look at the company's goals and the upside of the business plan.

"A properly written business plan also includes a strong interjection from its management and is professionally written," Trimble adds.

REMEMBER

15. A business plan is a planning and selling tool.
16. A business plan should be realistic and identify your company's strong and weak points with feasible solutions.
17. A business plan keeps your company headed in the right direction while providing you, your management and investors with a broad and realistic perspective of goals.
18. Sales will be lower and costs will be higher then you expect, so anticipate this in your business plan.
19. Practice presenting your plan.
20. Use it or lose it!

CHAPTER 5

Financing a Business

One of the biggest obstacles to starting a business is finding capital to get it off the ground. To aggressively pursue capital, you must be creative in your search for sources. Start-up and operating costs are high because of your need for research, developing your product, manufacturing or purchasing your inventory, marketing and advertising budgets, office supplies, payroll, rent, even your own living expenses. Your business may not generate enough profit to support itself, for months or even years, so you'll have to find a source from which to borrow.

Expensive and inexpensive businesses

There are many different types of businesses ranging from manufacturing to service and retail. Some businesses require only a small amount of start-up capital while others may require substantial sums to start and operate. Manufacturing businesses involve expensive areas such as research and development, equipment, raw materials and highly skilled labor. Retail businesses generally have lower operating costs, but initial costs of inventory, leasing space, display units and labor add up. On the other hand, service businesses typically require almost no initial capital if you can start the business out of your home. Other businesses with low capital requirements are ones with direct multi-level marketing such as Amway, Mary Kay and Avon.

Where to find capital

Consider many different sources when searching for capital to start your business. All investors have a universal motive—they want to make money. It is your job to convince an investor why your company is a good investment from his or her point of view. Prospective investors are among your many business and personal contacts—your attorney, accountant, banker, even friends and family. Begin your search at the library, where you will find trade magazines showing how other start-up companies found capital. Then, visit your local Small Business Administration and trade associations for your industry. The more you network, the better your chances to find what you need.

When looking for financing, don't approach your best prospects first. Instead, call on your long shots and practice giving your presentation to them. You might as well work out the rough spots in your presentation before you approach the sources who have the most potential to invest or loan the capital you need.

Friends and relatives

Accepting funds from family or friends is a complicated issue and one that has both helped and severed relationships. Use caution! On one hand, if you don't invite your friends and family to invest, and your business succeeds, they could resent you withholding a fruitful opportunity. Yet, if you do use their capital, and the business is a money-loser, they may blame you. First and foremost, never accept a large amount of capital from someone, friend or family member, who cannot afford to lose it. It is not worth the risk. The best advice I can offer is to invite friends and family to invest in your business only after it is out of its preliminary stages.

Private investors

The majority of start-up ventures are funded by private investors. These people are generally successful business people who are willing to and can afford to explore risky ventures. A private investor, if you are fortunate enough to find one, may serve as an excellent mentor and may know additional sources of capital.

Banking institutions

Loaning money is the business of banks—they earn interest on borrowed money. If you are a safe credit risk, and the bank believes your business will generate enough income and cash flow to meet the interest obligations on the loan, or you have the assets to repay the loan should your business fail, then you may qualify for all the capital you need. Of course, many banks require that you already be operating, and want to see tax returns dating back three years for you and your business, plus financial statements proving your business is profitable. Of course, these requirements rule out all new business owners who need capital to start their business, so broaden your options by developing working relationships with several banks.

Venture capital

One common source for capital is the venture capital firm. Many venture capital firms specialize in one particular industry, such as high-tech or pharmaceutical. Venture capital relationships are not the most desirable, as you lose some ownership interest in your business. Venture capitalists are "in-your-face" people—they do not invest and sit back, letting you go about your business as you please. They will want to be involved with your decision-making, regardless of what they tell you in the beginning.

Venture capitalists who invest in your company believe your business will grow substantially and pay a healthy return. They look for companies that have the potential, within three to five years, of providing an exit strategy for the investor. They want to see their way in and also need to be able to see their way out.

Exit strategies are any one of the following: a public offering, selling the company, merging with a larger company, or the company generates enough cash flow to buy the investors out. To successfully negotiate with a venture capitalist, you need to understand his or her specific goals and demonstrate how your company will earn a profit in the future.

Venture capitalist Bill Trimble explains the importance of an exit strategy in a business plan: "Before funding a company, we need to be able to see an exit strategy—a two-year window. If we can't clearly see an exit point, we won't pursue the business.

"We understand that no business will be fully developed in only two years," Trimble adds. "Especially businesses that are product-oriented or have developed new technology—they often take much longer than two years just to find a market niche. When this is the case, we are only interested if we believe that company will be successful enough to allow us the liquidity we might want down the road."

Down the road

Once your business has grown, you can find capital for expansion through franchising your business. Franchising provides your company with income and inexpensive expansion. If you franchise, you sell others the right to operate your business, sell your products and use your company name and logo. For a fee, you provide guidance and training on operating their franchises, advertising and marketing. A business with a marketable name and an easily duplicated concept can successfully attract franchisees.

Initial public offerings

Another way to raise capital, down the road, is by taking your company public. This isn't something to walk into casually. You should be especially cautious if you lack experience running a publicly held company, for it's a very complicated process. Being a public company requires making information about business dealings and holdings available to the stockholders, putting together a board of directors and taking on many new liabilities. It is very complex, but offers many advantages. For example, you and your investors could receive a large return for your initial investment.

Another reason to go public is to boost your company's image—projecting it as a stable and successful company. Going public is also the cheapest source of financing and it can also provide your business with a great deal of capital. This capital is equity financing, not debt financing—you don't have to pay your stockholders interest.

Keep in mind, as a publicly held company, you will have two types of customers. The first will be the customers who buy your product. The others are the stock market and Wall Street analysts who can make or break your business with their projections. You have to keep all of your customers happy to succeed!

Persistence pays off

After a few years, I felt it was time to move my business out of my garage. Unfortunately, I needed all the money my business was earning to buy materials, pay my employees and, what little was left, to support myself. There was no excess money, yet I needed nearly $20,000 to lease a suitable office and warehouse. So, off I went to half a dozen banks in search of a loan. At each one, I was literally thrown out for wasting the banker's time. I was 20 years old and, hard as I tried, no one gave me a chance to tell them about my wonderful business. My undeniable youth and lack of collateral seemed insurmountable handicaps.

Around this time, I enrolled in a finance class at a local community college. One class featured a banker as a guest lecturer. After class, I followed him to the parking lot so I could tell him about my business. But when I tried to introduce myself, he kept on walking. In desperation, I threw myself between him and his car door. He sighed, "Can I help you?"

I replied, "You told my class you wanted to help out, but when I tried to ask you for advice, you ignored me!"

His impassive look changed to an apologetic one and he handed me his business card. "Give me a call at the bank."

Soon, in my best suit, I was telling him about my business. I was very surprised when he said yes to a loan for the $20,000 I needed! Years later, the same banker became a member of my board of directors. Recently, I asked him why he gave me a loan that could have proved risky. He laughed, "Anybody with nerve enough to corner me in a parking lot is bound to succeed!" Bankers know that you lend to people not businesses.

I recommend dealing with a banker, not a bank. Build a relationship with the person and if necessary, continue to do business with him or her, should he or she leave to work for a different bank. I followed my banker, as he changed jobs, to three different banks. I did this because I didn't want to start all over again with a replacement. Banking relationships are based on honesty and credibility—something that is developed over a long period of time.

If you have a banker who you enjoy doing business with, do everything you can to stick with him or her. To do this, maintain a good relationship by treating him or her as well as you treat your customers. Call your banker often—with the good news and bad news. Help your banker do a good job by offering more information than he or she asks for.

Before your banker pays a visit to your company, prepare in advance and provide him or her with a formal agenda and outline for the meeting. After the visit, follow up with a letter recapping the issues you discussed. If you make your banker's job easier, he or she will not complain and will enjoy doing business with you.

REMEMBER

21. Don't approach your best prospects first—call on your long-shots and practice giving your presentation to them.
22. Accepting funds from family or friends requires much thought. Do not accept large amounts of money from friends and family who cannot afford the risk.
23. Investors have a universal motive—to make money.
24. Investors are always interested in knowing specific exit strategies—ways they can get out of the investment in the future. Exit strategies are any one of the following: a public offering, selling the company, merging with a larger company, or the company generates enough cash flow to buy the investors out.
25. When you are rejected for financing, find out why, then ask for suggestions of other people or institutions you could pursue.
26. When applying for a loan or searching for investors, always ask for more money than you really need. You can use the extra insurance because there is nothing worse than having to go back to your source asking for more money.

CHAPTER 6

Organizing the Business

When starting your new business, you will have to decide how to organize it. Will you take on a partner, a group of partners or will you organize it alone? Will you incorporate the business or make it a sole proprietorship? These are important questions to ask yourself. As always, consult your attorney before making a choice and for information regarding filings that may be required.

Being a sole proprietor

If you feel you can operate your business alone and obtain proper insurance, you don't want to spend the time or money to incorporate, you may choose to operate as a sole proprietorship or be aware that a sole proprietor has personal liability for all the debts of the company.

As a sole proprietor, you will do business under an assumed name—DBA (doing business as). For example, "The Acme Manufacturing Company."

Organizing as a corporation

Organizing your business as a corporation has many advantages. Most importantly, you'll have limited liability—only to the extent of

31

the assets of the corporation (assuming you meet certain requirements of law). While a general partner or sole proprietor is generally liable, if you organize as a corporation and properly document all transactions, maintain corporate records and don't co-mingle your personal funds with corporate funds, you won't be personally liable to creditors in the event of a lawsuit against the corporation. You can, however, lose the value of the corporation.

Organizing as a corporation requires the company to pay two layers of taxation—if the company has earnings. The corporation must pay tax, then after earnings are distributed to shareholders, they, too, must pay tax. On the other hand, a partnership does not pay tax. The partners pay tax as individuals—one layer of taxation.

According to Michael K.L. Wager, partner and member of the Corporate and Securities Practice Group with the Cleveland, Ohio, law firm of Benesch, Friedlander, Coplan and Aronoff, the best vehicle for a start-up entity may be to file as an S Corporation, "particularly if you think the company is going to be profitable from its inception," the attorney says. "When your business is profitable, and you want to protect your personal assets—you will want to incorporate. But if you want to avoid paying the two levels of taxation, you should go to your accountant and consider the benefits of an S Corporation. As an S Corporation, you have the benefit of flow-through taxation—meaning you are taxed only at the individual level, not the corporate level. Plus you have the limited liability of a shareholder of the corporation.

Establishing the game rules for a partnership

If you are not organizing your business alone, a partnership organization is the other option. A partnership is particularly useful for the following reasons: You can, by the partnership agreement, determine the relative rights and obligations of your partners. Statutes for partnerships under most state laws have very few limitations; therefore, the rights and obligations of you and your partners will be governed by a limited or general partnership agreement.

If a partnership is your choice, you must decide whether you and your partners will be equals. Will they work in the business, or will they be passive investors while you are the active participant? Will your partners invest equal amounts of capital?

There are two types of partnerships—general and limited. In a general partnership, each partner has personal, unlimited liability for the obligations of the partnership—from the company's creditors to anybody else in the world who has a claim against the business entity.

A limited partnership consists of at least one general partner and one limited partner. In this type of partnership, the general partner (or partners, if there are more than one) is fully liable for the partnership's obligations. The general partner also has control over the business, while the limited partners have limited liability—only to the extent of the amount of their capital contribution. Limited partners also have limited rights of control—how much active involvement they can have in the business.

A limited partnership can be used as a vehicle to raise funds. While the limited partners have the advantage of making an investment without becoming generally liable for the debts and obligations of the company, the organizer, who is the general partner, remains generally liable.

According to Wager, whose practice is primarily securities and corporate counseling with an emphasis on corporate finance, mergers and acquisitions, "There's no requirement that a *general* partnership must have any sort of written agreement to be legally considered a partnership.

"Nevertheless, for their own protection, the partners should enter into a partnership agreement that spells out their respective rights and obligations," Wager continues. "For a limited partnership, there are a number of formalities required for the formation and operation. If you are considering either of these forms of doing business, you should consult with an attorney concerning the requirements of law and business stratagems.

"There is one golden rule if you have a partner—that you must have a written agreement," he adds. "Anytime two or more parties engage in a business together, they should have an agreement which governs their rights and obligations during the operation of the business and how they exit or unwind their business. The agreement should address what percentage of the company each of you will own. You will both be general partners unless you specifically identify your partner as a limited partner and file the appropriate documents with the state."

Wager recommends having a carefully crafted agreement for passive investors as well. "They, too, need an agreement as to what their rights and obligations will be and what their exit mechanisms will be.

"And if you are raising capital from outside investors who don't want general liability, you must comply with the limited partnership statute in your state (or the corporate statute) so they have limited liability either as shareholders, if you are a corporation, or as limited partners, if you are registered as a partnership."

Depending on the business location, some states require the filing of a partnership certificate for general partnerships, while most states require the filing of a partnership certificate for a limited partnership, in addition to several other formalities.

The partner compatibility test

Are you sure you really want a partner? What is going to define the roles of the partners? Who is going to decide who is in charge? Is it a 50-50 partnership? If your purpose is to find a partner to operate the business with you, compatibility is an important issue, although it is always a good thing to be compatible with all of your partners— whether they are general or limited. There can only be one boss and when two egos are involved, it can be complicated.

When Bill LeVine, founder of PIP printing, considers a partner, he first examines the individual's background, what he or she does and his or her desire for the future.

"Partnerships are difficult," he says. "This is part of the reason why franchising has its problems—the franchisee invests in your company and you invest in him—it is truly a partnership." "The royalty you collect is the equivalent of a dividend as a partner or an investor in your business. In exchange, you provide certain services and the franchisee has his obligations, too. But for it to work, both parties must understand what their responsibilities are. This is why it is very important to discuss these matters upfront."

According to Bill Trimble, president and CEO of venture capital firm W.A.T. Capital Corp., the best way to own a business is to *own* it. "My philosophy on partners is very simple," he explains. "When you have a partner, you will have twice as many potential problems. Likewise, if there are four partners, you'll have that many more sources for potential problems. So, the more partners you have in a private company, the more ongoing grief you are going to deal with.

"Furthermore, liquidity is impossible unless you have a shotgun agreement," he adds.

The shotgun agreement (buy-sell)

Breaking up a partnership is similar to a divorce—sometimes even worse. This is why I recommend including a shotgun clause in every partnership or shareholder agreement. Similar to a marriage, two parties who own a business together can become very bitter when it is time to dissolve their relationship. A shotgun agreement is analogous to a prenuptial agreement, because it has predetermined terms.

The shotgun agreement allows both parties the ability to easily dissolve the partnership or corporation at any time. For example, if Jane owns a business with Sam, and Jane wants to end the business relationship, she exercises the shotgun agreement by offering Sam a fair price for the business. Sam has the option of selling the business to Jane or buying the business from her for the same price. Sam has an advantage because he is able to choose which option he wants first. If Sam decides to sell out to Jane, he will be out of the business completely, and she must buy. Likewise, if he wants to keep the business, he must pay Jane what she offered, and she will no longer be an owner. The shotgun agreement is a one-shot deal.

Put up or shut up!

Shotgun agreement clauses are important to include in every partnership or shareholder agreement. Though the clause may be considered a drastic way to resolve a problem and end a business, it is the quickest and easiest way to do so. In the unlikely case that neither party chooses to buy the other out, the business will be sold and the proceeds divided.

Seek assistance in writing the contract from an attorney who specializes in business transactions. Don't write a contract without help.

REMEMBER

27. When starting your new business, you will have to decide how you are going to organize it.
28. In a general partnership each partner has personal, unlimited liability for the obligations of the partnership—from the company's creditors to anybody else in the world who has a claim against the business entity.
29. Check with your attorney about appropriate filings.
30. Decide upfront if you want to organize as a limited partnership, a general partnership or as a sole proprietor. Will you incorporate the business?
31. Partner compatibility is an important issue to consider—look at the individual's background, as well as his or her goals.
32. For a partnership to work, both parties should have a clear understanding of their rights and obligations to the business.
33. Partners should have an agreement that spells out their respective rights, obligations and the exit mechanism—this is a golden rule!
34. A shotgun agreement, which allows either party to easily dissolve the relationship at any time, is analogous to a prenuptial agreement, because it has predetermined terms.
35. Don't write a contract for a partner or investor without the assistance of a professional.

CHAPTER 7

The Business of Running a Business

When you start a business, you'll undoubtedly spend a great deal of time developing a business plan, hiring employees, finding capital, marketing, selling and much more. But there are many more details to attend to when running a business. The business of running a business includes tedious tasks you may not enjoy, but that are necessary. If these items are put off, they can turn into massive headaches down the road. You may even face legal trouble if some are not completed.

These necessary details include: insurance, worker's compensation, state regulatory requirements, licenses, permits, leases, contracts with suppliers and manufacturers, employee records, payroll and financial record-keeping.

Getting locked into a long-term contract, lease or agreement of any type is not the best way to start a new business. These could restrict your growth if you find better and less expensive opportunities with someone else. Your business may quickly outgrow the supplier, manufacturer or space you are obligated to, so think about your future before signing any papers! Also, have your attorney look over every contract in advance of signing.

The owner of a business must be protected in case of a lawsuit, so therefore you will need several different insurance coverages. For example, as the owner, you must be covered for liability purposes. This expense cannot be overlooked in case of injury to an employee or customer. Even if you are just leasing your space, you need property insurance. If both you and your landlord have property coverage, include what is called a "mutual waiver of subrogation" in your lease. This protects you from being sued by the landlord's insurer for damages you are responsible for. You might want to consult your mentor, attorney or board of directors before signing a policy. They will help you choose the best coverage and the proper amount that you need. Carefully select the insurer you do business with, to avoid insurance companies that are not in good financial health.

The most tedious of the tedious may well be worker's compensation insurance requirements. This varies from state to state, so consult your insurance professional to find out how to file correctly.

State regulatory requirements also vary. Many states offer a free or inexpensive booklet that will guide you through the process of applying for a license or meeting permit requirements. For further information, contact your local chamber of commerce or the small-business office in your city.

You must maintain thorough employee records and keep a running written record of commendations, reprimands, attendance, salary history and bonuses relating to the employee. Each employee's file should also include a job description and a written agreement that they have signed that says you may change their hours and job description if necessary. Otherwise, if you do this without their written consent and they quit as a result, they may be entitled to unemployment benefits, giving you higher premiums. Keep this agreement in the employee's file, and be certain to give him or her a copy. For a variety of issues that may arise in the future, every record regarding your employees is important to keep. Foremost, these records will be useful if you are ever sued for wrongful termination.

Financial records are obviously important—especially if you are audited by the IRS! A competent accountant and bookkeeper can help you maintain your records and create a balance sheet. Believe me, every one of your investors will be very interested in knowing your financial status—on a regular basis!

You may not be excited after reading about these details that must be taken care of—but they are part of running a business. Exciting or not, they need your attention.

REMEMBER

36. Getting locked into a long-term contract, lease or agreement of any type (with a supplier, manufacturer or landlord) is not the best way to start a new business. They can restrict your growth or you may find better and less expensive opportunities with someone else.
37. Your business will need liability and property insurance.
38. Consult your attorney, mentor or board to help you choose the best coverage before signing any policies.
39. Carefully select the insurer you do business with, to avoid insurance companies that are not in good financial health.
40. Consult your insurance professional when applying for worker's compensation.
41. State regulatory requirements such as applying for a license or permit vary. Contact your local chamber of commerce or the small-business office in your city for assistance.
42. Maintain thorough employee records and keep a running written record of commendations, reprimands, attendance, salary history, job descriptions and bonuses relating to the employee. Include in this file, a signed, written agreement with your employees that says you may change their hours and or change their job description if necessary. These records will be useful if you are ever sued for wrongful termination.
43. Keep good financial records. If you are audited, you'll need them!

CHAPTER 8

Being a Self-Motivator and Motivating Your People

As a business owner, you face two critical issues: keeping yourself motivated and motivating your employees. Without self-motivation, it is impossible to motivate others. And unless your employees are motivated, it will be difficult for your company to succeed.

The importance of setting goals

Every day, you must wake up with a high energy level, looking forward to starting your day at the office. No one tells the owner of a business what to do, so you must be your own manager and motivator. This can be done every day by setting goals for yourself—both short-term and long-term goals you can reach. You should never set goals that you know you will never reach, because it will cause constant disappointment. Everybody gets self-satisfaction from accomplishing and achieving goals. Even you!

When writing a list, no one knows better than you what needs to get done. Every morning, you should put together a written list of what you want to accomplish that day. Include specific telephone calls you want to make and letters you want to write. You may include long-term goals, such as sales projections or plans for expansion. I list both my long-term and short-term goals every day. When I accomplish a goal, I check it off my list. Before I leave work at day's end, I move unfinished items to the next day's list. Each goal checked off gives you the energy you need to be motivated. No matter what is on your list, completion brings self-satisfaction. Remember, success is only a matter of accomplishing goals that you have set for yourself.

Motivating your employees

As the leader of your company, you ensure the survival and success of your business by motivating your employees. This is your responsibility as the leader of your organization. You move your company forward when you go to work every day with enthusiasm, because enthusiasm is contagious. Catch it!

You, as leader, must clearly communicate to your employees any specific objectives you want them to meet. Help them meet these goals by providing them with the equipment and the direction they need. You can constantly remind your employees of the company's goals. How do you motivate your employees to meet your objectives? You can offer them incentives—monetary compensation, stock, profit sharing, etc., as well as the more important intangibles such as recognition and status. If you make people feel good about themselves, they will work a lot harder for you than if you use the big stick. People are going to respect you and work harder for you if you treat them with mutual respect. Compensation goes a long way and you will get more out of your people through appreciation by giving them the pat on the back that they deserve. People *work* for money, but they *want* recognition.

How you should compensate monetarily also depends on the level of your employee's position within the company. Most entry-level employees would prefer to be compensated with cash—they are in for the short-haul and probably are not interested in promises for the future. Employees who are in for the long-haul are ones who expect to be treated fairly when it comes to wages. If they are under-compensated, they will lose their motivation to work hard and can cause more damage to company morale than you can imagine. The movers and shakers within your organization are motivated by monetary compensation as well as the chance to grow and make a difference for the company. They can be motivated through compensation, including bonuses based on performance and career advancement.

As the founder of California Closets, I was ultimately responsible for every aspect of the company. No matter how good or bad things were, my responsibility was to motivate my people to go on. In tough times, I pushed my employees and franchisees to work even harder. When business is bad, you need to be twice as good! It was my job is to keep everyone's spirits high. I was careful to always set reasonable goals for my employees. A goal must be attainable! A goal that's impossible to reach will surely discourage your employees.

Entrepreneurs not only are dreamers, but doers and goal-setters. They create ideas but they don't stop there. They take action. As the leader of a company, you, too, must have vision, direction, un-bounded energy, tremendous drive, a strong desire for success and many goals. This action will never stop until your business is either closed or sold.

Examples of goals

Sales goals
Personal goals (exercise and personal health)
Productivity goals
Expansion goals
Marketing goals

REMEMBER

44. Without self-motivation, it is impossible to motivate others.
45. As the owner of a business, you won't have someone to supervise you or to tell you what to do, so you must be your own manager and motivator. Every day set goals for yourself—both short-term and long-term.
46. Visualizing your goals helps you define the steps that need to be taken in order to achieve the goal.
47. Enthusiasm is contagious. Catch it!
48. As the company leader, communicate to your employees specific goals you want them to meet, and provide them with the necessary direction and materials.
49. Compensation goes a long way, but you will get more out of your people through appreciation by giving them the pat on the back that they deserve. People work for money, but they want recognition and acceptance.

CHAPTER 9

The Entrepreneurial Ego

The longer I'm in the business, the more I'm convinced there's an entrepreneurial ego—the drive to be successful. It takes a special type of person to go his or her own way and defy the crowd. A successful entrepreneur maintains the self-confidence necessary to accomplish a goal no matter how many people say it can't be done.

Yet there is a tremendous difference between having an ego—everybody's got one—and being egotistical. The ego can be negative unless channeled in the right direction, while being egotistical can be very destructive. A person with an entrepreneurial ego is driven with a burning desire to build something. When this desire is channeled in the right direction, the entrepreneurial ego takes over, providing enormous drive.

It takes a certain amount of ego to be a boss and, in this capacity, have the confidence required to make decisions. Let's face it, as the owner of your own business, it's your money that's on the line. So when push comes to shove, if you don't have the guts to take decisive action when it's demanded, nothing will get done. So, while you may seek the opinion of your associates, it's still you who must act upon the input you receive and make the final decision.

The destructive ego

Don't let your ego stand in the way of success. When you make a mistake, admit it. My father used to tell me, "Remember, Neil, you are never too slick to be greased." I realized it is more important to worry about *what* is right—not *who* is right. If you make a mistake, the first step to correct it is to admit it. Tell your colleagues, "I'm sorry. I thought I was doing the right thing." What will their reaction be? Probably, they will admire you for your ability to admit it. After all, most people value humility. If you choose to defend a mistake, your employees will lose respect for you. Everyone makes mistakes—just don't compound an error by trying to defend it.

Don't let ego prevent you from asking questions or seeking advice. If I don't understand something, I'll say, "Nobody wants to ask, so I will...explain this to me." The worst thing you can do is not ask a question if you have one. If you don't understand something, you're put at a disadvantage. Plus, your colleagues will appreciate you asking them questions. You could say, "I don't understand how we can make this work. Can you please explain it to me?"

Movers and shakers

True entrepreneurs are movers and shakers. They make things happen. No question about it, entrepreneurs must be bold and courageous and be willing to put themselves on the line. Ideas are a dime a dozen, but men and women who implement them are priceless. A person with a good idea but no conviction is much worse off than another with a bad idea who has conviction. A successful entrepreneur doesn't need a great personality—but he or she must have tenacity, drive and commitment.

No "overnight" success

Those without the entrepreneurial ego often give up at the first sign of adversity. They throw in the towel and go on to something else rather than hurdling the obstacles. A true entrepreneur has unrelenting self-confidence regardless of naysayers. Entrepreneurs starting a business, put their life on the line; they can't afford fear of failure.

Every entrepreneur faces resistance and skepticism at first. But they must not give up at the first sign of adversity. If the owner doesn't believe in his or her business, how can anyone else believe in it? Of course, successful entrepreneurs do believe in their business—with all their heart and soul. They may come across as egotistical when people mistake their supreme self-confidence for arrogance.

The ideal entrepreneur treads a fine line between never losing belief and maintaining humility. Achieving this balance is no easy matter.

REMEMBER

50. Don't let your ego stand in the way of success.
51. Don't let your ego prevent you from asking questions or seeking advice.
52. Worry about what's right—not who's right.
53. Be bold and courageous; be willing to put your business life on the line.
54. Visualize what you want, then go after it.
55. A person with an entrepreneurial ego is driven with a burning desire to build something.
56. A true entrepreneur has unrelenting self-confidence necessary to accomplish goals, regardless of naysayers. An entrepreneur who starts a business can't afford fear of failure.

CHAPTER 10

Success is a Matter of Luck: Ask Any Failure!

As the owner of a business, you will have your share of trying times. You may even ask yourself, "Why am I doing this? Enough is enough!" This is a common feeling among entrepreneurs, which you should expect to have from time to time. But successful entrepreneurs aren't affected by adversities—they have the desire to make their business work no matter what it requires. They never give up. They bounce back with more energy each time. A common response among entrepreneurs is that the harder things get, the harder they work.

It's no bed of roses

Running a small or medium-size business is not easy. In most cases, the owner has invested his or her own money in the business. An executive at a large company, such as General Motors, doesn't face the same challenges you face—he doesn't have his life savings and his house mortgaged for his business. When you own your own business, you are at risk. Your money is on the line. Your family and employees depend on its success. Even your future is at stake. Why do you stick with it? Because you have a dream, a dream of where you want to be in your life, and you're willing to work for it. You have to want it more than most anything else.

For the first six months, the entrepreneur works hard, and things may go well. After six months, things become more difficult. The business is growing, yet it isn't making money, and he or she may become depressed. The first two years of operation involve the combined pressures of raising capital, building a business and earning a profit. Most businesses don't turn a profit until the second or third year, when things settle down. Once the business is off the ground, many owners realize that second thoughts just come with the territory.

Family discussions

Having a family is a great responsibility, but so is owning and growing your business. You and your family will have to make many sacrifices. There will be many pressures on your family—all resulting from the business—such as less money to live on and less time you are at home. Small business owners don't have as much time for family and friends as they may have had at one time, and are often too tired to go out. You will miss your kid's soccer games, family potlucks, and a wedding or two (hopefully not your own).

So, if you have a family, before you start a business, sit down with each member and discuss every sacrifice that needs to be made. There's nothing worse than starting a business that will eventually destroy your family. This happens when family members are not aware of the time and effort that will be required of you and them. If a family isn't supportive of a business, it could destroy the family *and* the business. I have seen many marriages break up over a business and I have seen many businesses fail because of a bad marriage.

Second thoughts

Never, never, never give up. A tremendous belief in yourself is your business's best asset. Many times I considered giving up. I saw my friends who worked for other people, having more time to spend with their friends and families. They didn't worry about their work day and night. I still envy them, but I've had the gratification of building and operating my own business, in spite of sacrifices and challenges that I continue to face.

Sorry to say, you must be willing to make sacrifices. This is not easy—it is harder than having a regular job! There is nothing wrong with working for someone else and working 8 a.m. to 5 p.m. Most people are satisfied working for someone else for a 40-hour work week. They like leaving the office with nothing to worry about. Believe me, it would be nice to be able to go home at 5 p.m. and leave my work at the office! The hours you will work when you own a business will be a lot longer, and you're never off—even if you are at home or on vacation! You will think about work all the time!

Owning a business can be a big worry. It's just not for everybody. It is a 24-hours-a-day, seven-days-a-week, 52 weeks-a-year deal, not something you can turn on and off. Not everyone has what it takes to be a successful entrepreneur and that's okay. For awhile, it may seem that the more you tend your business, the more monstrous its appetite for your time. After two or three years, you could have more life away from the office. But are you certain that owning a business is what you really want? Do you and your family have the commitment it requires?

REMEMBER

57. When you own your own business, you take a tremendous risk. Your money is on the line, your family and employees depend on its success, even your future depends on it.
58. The first two years of operation are the most difficult for an owner because of the pressures of raising capital, building the business and earning a profit.
59. You need to have a tremendous belief in yourself and be committed to your business. An element of risk is involved in every business, but manage these risks by understanding what they are.
60. If you have a spouse and children, before you start a business, sit down with them and discuss every sacrifice that needs to be made. You need their support to succeed!

CHAPTER 11

Beware of the Doomsayers

As a business owner, you will face many obstacles. A difficult one is a doomsayer. A doomsayer is an acquaintance, friend—even a family member—who predicts your failure. These doubting Thomases don't want you to own a business or to succeed.

Doomsayers criticize your hopes and dreams because they don't have their own. Jealousy can bring out the worst in people. It is easier to be negative and say you are going to fail than to be positive and support your idea. Disregard what they say; don't let them damage your self-confidence. You'll always have to deal with people who envy your accomplishments. They envy your courage, determination and self-esteem. They may even mistake your enthusiasm for arrogance. Most doomsayers have never done anything on their own. They have not started their own business and don't know the first thing about how to do it. Hold on to your hopes and dreams and work hard for them.

My nay-sayers

When I was 17 and trying to start a business, I faced my share of doomsayers. My business was growing and I desperately needed capital for expansion. Of course, I was young and my appearance was not professional—my hair was halfway down my back and there were holes in my jeans. Most banks are used to dealing with older, more sophisticated people. I did not meet their expectations.

It was very disheartening when I walked into banks only to be confronted by bankers angry with me for wasting their time! Twice my age, making $30,000 to $40,000 a year, they envied me for starting my own business. They tried their best to discourage me from expanding my small business, but no matter what they said, I never stopped trying, because I knew they were wrong.

I had a very bad experience with one particular bank manager in Los Angeles. After I explained my business and showed photographs of my work, the manager told me that my business was not a viable one and he didn't do business with kids. "Why are you here wasting my time?" he asked me. I left his office, my face flushed with anger.

Years later, after my business had expanded and was well-known, banks approached me to do business with them. One afternoon, a bank representative came to see me and as he started his pitch, he handed me a business card. I realized he was from the same bank that had been so rude to me when I was starting out. I mentioned the name of the manager I encountered years earlier, and asked if he was still there. I learned from the rep that this same manager had been promoted to vice president. I called my secretary and asked her to pull out an article from *The Wall Street Journal* that had praised my business. I handed the article to the representative and exclaimed, "Give this article to your vice president, and tell him I don't do business with people who throw me out of their banks!"

That manager predicted people would never pay to have their closets organized. Well, he was no visionary! My company has filled a basic need for thousands of satisfied customers in what is today a $500 million industry!

The Holiday Inn story

In the summer of 1951, while on a family vacation in Washington, D.C., Kemmons Wilson was appalled to see that lodgings available along the way from his native Tennessee were dirty, cramped and overpriced. He recognized the need for more comfortable, standardized and economical accommodations for travelers around the country. Returning to his hometown, Memphis, with the thought fresh in his mind, he vowed to do something about it.

"The experience," he says with a frown, "was so bad that as soon as I got back to Memphis I decided to build the right kind of motel, one that would have all the things my family missed on that trip.

"I told my friends about my concept and my plan to build a chain of 400 motels," he recalls. "Everybody I talked to thought I was crazy."

Wilson's friends tried to talk him out of going forward with the concept. If Wilson had let the doomsayers talk him out of his idea, he'd have given up very early. Instead, he disregarded the criticism and pursued his dream. Fortunately, one banker believed in Wilson's concept and loaned him the $350,000 he needed to build the first Holiday Inn.

The first inn opened in Memphis in 1952, and 20 months later, three more were built, each on a major highway approach into the city. Today, there are more than 1,600 Holiday Inns in 51 different countries. It's a good thing Wilson didn't let his doomsayers discourage him from pursuing his goal!

REMEMBER

61. Doomsayers criticize your hopes and dreams. Disregard what they say and don't let them damage your self-confidence.
62. Do not become angry with a doomsayer. Stay in control of the situation and play by your rules.

CHAPTER 12

Uncharted Waters

If the service or product your company offers is revolutionary, be prepared to travel a bumpy road with many detours. Developing your business will be adventurous and exciting, and will exercise your creativity! It's a great advantage to have a unique service or product not already available to your customers.

Disadvantages of offering a new concept

A product that's new or different has no competition. But the uncharted waters you travel present some difficulties. For example, you have no one to teach you what mistakes to avoid. You may find it challenging to establish credibility with customers, suppliers, manufacturers and bankers. A company selling something new is forced to relate the product to the customer's personal needs, wants or desires. It was up to me to convince people who had never heard of such a service, to use California Closet Company.

I prefer offering something new and different to customers rather than competing with established companies. The rewards can be much greater.

Disadvantages of offering an existing concept

There are disadvantages to owning a business with an existing concept already offered by other companies. If your company shares the market with competition, it could be difficult to develop a strong customer base of your own. You must develop a unique selling proposition to differentiate your company and product from the competition's. You must convince your potential customers why your product or service is better than the competition's. Perhaps it stands out in some way, for example, by offering a lower price or better customer service. If you succeed, you can claim your own territory in the marketplace.

When I ventured into uncharted waters

I encountered difficulties in the early years because I was young and inexperienced. I started California Closets as a teenager with no track record. I couldn't say, "I have done this before," so it was difficult for me to convince others what I could do. A person with 15 or 20 years in business has an easier time finding financing, employees and customers. Even several years after the business became known around the country, I faced obstacles because of my youth. People thought of me as a kid even after I'd been in business nearly 10 years.

I had no competition for the first few years I was in business. Previously, no one had operated a business that specialized in closet organization before me. Although some carpenters did do the same work, they did not have the resources or materials my company did. I used this to my advantage. I generated publicity through talk shows, news broadcasts and magazine and newspaper articles promoting my unique concept. The media convinced my potential customer base of the benefits of my product.

When interviewed by the media, I would say, "Just think about your closet at home. Your shoes are all over the floor and there is never enough space for your clothes. Wouldn't you like to do something about it?" I appeared on local news broadcasts, showing the viewing audience film footage of a closet before and after being organized by my company. I also used my youth as an advantage. I promoted myself as a bright, young entrepreneur who had started a business. This attracted more press coverage for the company, which in turn gave me credibility as a businessman.

Whether you are inexperienced or seasoned, your product or service should benefit your customer in some way. If you are fortunate enough to offer a product that is unique, you could have an exciting future ahead, yet there's nothing wrong with a company that sells an existing concept. What's important is that your product or service and customer service be better than the competition in some way. Either way, your product should be something your customer needs. Get the customer to focus on what makes you unique and different.

PIP and uncharted waters

Bill LeVine, founder of PIP printing company, started the quick-print industry in 1967. An operating printer who owned Postal Press in Los Angeles, California, LeVine created the concept when he discovered the "ITEK" camera at a trade show. He immediately envisioned the possibilities for the printing industry. Though he had a great concept, the hardest part of being first in a field was informing the public of his existence.

"Before we introduced 'quick print,' it was very costly and time-consuming to get a print job done," he explains. "It was an eight-step process just to make a plate for the printing press. This alone cost the customers $15 to $25, and they still had to get the copies made! Needless to say, this was not cost-effective, especially for smaller jobs!

"We offered a new service," he continues. "In 1967, PIP charged far less than anyone else, and took less time."

"My company was able to give the customer a high-quality print job for a low price," tells LeVine. "A customer didn't have to order 1,000 copies—he or she could order 100 copies for as little as $3.95. Plus, the job could be done immediately—we offered a two-step printing process, with a much higher quality than a mimeographed or dittoed copy.

"Before the quick-print process, a customer would have to schedule an appointment with a normal printer, drop off the job, and wait anywhere from three days to three weeks," recollects LeVine. "This was the case even to get a simple job done. Back then, printers scheduled their jobs. A customer could not walk in to a printer and wait for the job to be done that same day. My concept allowed customers to come in without an appointment, have a cup of coffee while they waited, and before they were even finished with the coffee, their 100-copy job was ready to go.

Though it was easy to convince customers that PIP's concept was better than the rest, there were still disadvantages to being the first in the quick-print industry.

"One problem we faced was that the chemicals we used were not perfected as they are today," recalls LeVine. "On some days, the chemicals weren't as good. The quality of the chemicals fluctuated with the weather conditions! Another disadvantage was we didn't have anyone to teach us how to trouble-shoot or how to write the manuals to teach the staff how the machines worked. The biggest one, however, was that it was difficult to find locations for the stores.

"Finding the best locations in the right areas took a lot of time and was difficult," he continues. "I had to negotiate the leases before I knew how well our stores could do."

Overall, LeVine had many more advantages by being the first. "We had a tremendous advantage over the other printers because we were able to produce the product with good quality quickly and for less money."

Being a pioneer in the industry, LeVine had to go to great lengths to get the customers to come to his store. "I did whatever I could to get people in the door," he tells. "People understood what printing was, but they didn't understand how they could get a few copies for a very low price in just a few minutes. Overall, it was an easy sale, and it took off like a bat out of hell!"

REMEMBER

63. It is more difficult to avoid mistakes if your concept is new, because you have no one to learn from. Yet, if your product is an existing concept, the market could be saturated, or it could be difficult to develop a strong customer base.
64. You must develop a unique selling proposition to differentiate your company and your product from the competition's.
65. If your concept is offered by other companies, your company must be different and stand out in some way, for example, by offering a lower price or better customer service.

CHAPTER 13

Finding a Mentor

When you first start your business, you need all the help you can get, and then some. Even if you went to college or business school, the classroom differs from the real world. Most of your professors were never out there "doing it." Theory by itself doesn't cut it—there's no substitute for hands-on experience. This is where a mentor becomes invaluable.

A qualified mentor is someone who has already experienced the same sort of thing you're trying to accomplish. He or she doesn't have to be directly involved in your business and may even work in another field. Ideally, this person should have started out small (like you), faced many of the same obstacles, and went on to succeed in his or her own business.

A mentor teaches you the ropes so you won't have to learn from your own mistakes. The lessons may be as basic as what to ask for when buying from a supplier, what quantities to order initially, or how to handle a dissatisfied customer. Additionally, your mentor is somebody to turn to when you're down after having a bad day.

Everybody likes to help the underdog

It is easy to find a mentor. All you have to do is be a little humble and ask for help. Most people are thrilled to mentor because it's

63

flattering. Everybody loves to have their opinion solicited—it's a real ego trip. In searching for a mentor, you discover that most people are receptive about giving their opinions, particularly when it helps a novice. Successful individuals enjoy helping new people in business because when they were young, someone probably helped them. It's like the saying, "What comes around goes around."

Although it may be easier for a young entrepreneur to find a mentor, old-timers can do it, too. Older people sometimes have problems finding mentors because they're embarrassed to ask for help. Don't allow false pride to keep you from asking for advice.

Choosing the right mentor

Every successful person is not automatically a good mentor, for several reasons. He or she may not have started a business from scratch, and this by itself could be grounds for disqualification. For instance, if a successful person was privileged—earned an MBA from Harvard, came from a well-to-do family, had a lot of financing available in the beginning or, in other words, didn't have to struggle or worry about the same everyday headaches you do—then this person may not be a good candidate.

Another poor candidate is someone older who started his or her business way back when. Times were different in those days and what worked then might not work for you. You want to find a mentor who has done things more recently, if possible, and particularly someone who is still in business. You don't want to consult someone who retired 10 or 15 years ago and is out of touch with today's marketplace. You need a person active in his or her business, even if it was started many years ago. This person will still be savvy about what's going on and what's happening.

Ideally, a mentor understands your business but is not directly involved and can therefore be objective. When people are in the heat of the day-to-day battles, they don't see things as clearly as when they have distance. Be aware—listen to your mentor's opinions and digest what you hear.

Be selective in choosing your mentor. You don't want a mentor who won't give you time. Don't choose a person difficult to get through to on the telephone, who is never in or won't promptly return your phone calls. You do want someone accessible.

My mentors

The year after I started my business, I took a small business management course at a local community college. That's where I met David Seigel, a marketing and sales professor. Before joining the faculty at Pierce College in the Los Angeles area, David started a large business in the mid-'50s with his four brothers, that developed, manufactured and sold the first commercial convertible couch.

David was the most popular professor on campus and would bend over backwards to help his students. He took a shine to me and quickly took me under his wing. Most of his advice focused on how I should market my product and find more customers.

My new mentor convinced me to clean up my act by cutting my hair, shaving my beard and mustache, and getting decent clothes. He told me, "If you want to build the business, you are going to have to start acting like a businessman. Play by the rules—don't buck the system!" We would meet once or twice a week to talk about obstacles I was running up against as a new business owner. David was a great mentor because he had been in business for many years, and could speak from experience. He understood the headaches, risks and the crises I endured as a business owner.

Other people's mentors

Doug Mellinger is the chairman and CEO of PRT Corp. of America, a New York-based company that specializes in the planning, implementation and knowledge transfer of advanced computer technology. Mellinger started his career as an entrepreneur while still a college student. "I discovered that my young age was an advantage," the entrepreneur explains. "Because I was young, people bent over backwards to help me and were very forgiving when I made mistakes.

"My mentors are completely responsible for the magnitude of the success I have achieved," Mellinger adds. "I wouldn't be where I am today were it not for my mentors. Plus, they are easy to find because everybody wants to be one!"

Having a board of directors

A board of directors is an inexpensive and easy way for you to utilize experienced people to help you make decisions and advise you what to do and, more importantly, what not to do.

A good board adds depth and knowledge, helping you solve problems relating to operations, strategy and other issues of your business. The compensation you give them is a modest expense if you consider what they would cost you as consultants!

The best board of directors is comprised of a collection of business associates including customers, bankers, consultants, accountants and attorneys. They should be able to help you with your weak areas. For example, if your weakness is marketing, select someone for your board who is an expert in this area. Inviting friends or relatives to sit on your board is not the best idea.

REMEMBER

66. Listen to your mentor.
67. Ask your mentor lots of questions and listen carefully. If you don't agree with what your mentor says, don't be afraid to discuss the issues and let him or her sell you on those ideas.
68. Express your gratitude to your mentor. Share your enthusiasm as well as your appreciation for what he or she has taught you.
69. Follow up with your mentor. Let your mentor share in your successes.
70. People support that which they help to create. When your mentor becomes involved, he or she can be very supportive. In the creative process of a new concept, people become more enthusiastic when they are involved.
71. Select a group of advisers to be your board of directors, whether official or not.
72. As your business grows, so do your needs for a mentor. In time you may outgrow your current one and need to graduate to somebody else. A growth business has many different stages, each of which may require a different mentor.
73. Having a board of directors is an inexpensive and easy way for you to utilize experienced people to help you make decisions.

CHAPTER 14

Turning Disadvantages Into Advantages

Along with the advantages come disadvantages every new business owner must face. These range from inexperienced staff to lack of customers or referrals. Fortunately, many negatives are also positives, often giving a small business the upperhand over its larger counterparts.

Advantages to having new employees

Your employees will be new and inexperienced when your company is young. They haven't yet learned their jobs, and will likely make many mistakes. Yet, the situation is not bleak. Your employees have one quality that workers for large companies lack—enthusiasm. They are excited because everything is new and the company is growing. They work as a team and feel like a family. Specific jobs may not be defined yet, but your employees are willing to do whatever it takes to make the company successful.

Large companies have a lot of fat—more staff than they need and a complex array of expensive benefits. It's difficult for large companies to level with their employees in a time of need. But, when your business is small, it's easy to be honest with your employees by informing them when you are have a bad month, cash flow problems, etc. They will be very understanding, and will work even harder to make the company more profitable.

Many business owners worry that because their business is small, they can't effectively compete with large companies. Nothing could be further from the truth. Small businesses avoid many problems experienced by large companies. As a business grows, so does its overhead, forcing the company to earn a wider gross profit margin.

Small businesses can be light on their feet and respond to the market by making changes quickly. Whatever the competitive advantage, it must be found, marketed and capitalized on.

Small businesses are usually more cost-efficient than the competition. A young company can charge less than the competition because layers of overhead haven't accumulated. Small business adaptability permits wider selection and customized service. It can take a large company up to five years to research and develop a product. Large companies are lethargic, political entities, relying on committees to decide every issue from marketing to product liability. How can a large company be flexible after it has spent hundreds of thousands of dollars on current products and services it cannot afford to change?

While your new business may lack credibility, it does have the advantage of starting with a clean reputation. As a new owner, you make sure every customer you serve is satisfied. Regardless of its high standards, when a company has been around for a while, inevitably it upsets some customers. New businesses do all they can to impress customers. Go beyond the call of duty every time you deal with a customer, because bad word-of-mouth spreads farther and faster than its counterpart.

My youth and inexperience

When I started California Closets, I had many disadvantages. No maturity. No experience. No capital or credibility. I didn't even have a client base. I took my youth and turned it into an advantage by seeking mentors from among the most experienced, successful people in the country. Surprisingly, many experienced business people bent over backwards to help me. All I had to do was ask! They expected nothing from me in return for the valuable advice they gave—they just got a kick out of helping. Successful, older people enjoy being around eager young people because they see a lot of themselves.

Customers also like to see young people succeed, and they enjoy helping any way they can. When the job is done right, with good customer service, customers want to support a young entrepreneur. Remember buying a 5-cent cup of lemonade from a neighbor's kid? People like to support the underdog and, face it, when you are young and in business, you're definitely the underdog! Success is attainable for every entrepreneur willing to work for it.

REMEMBER

74. Your employees have one valuable quality that others who work for large companies lack—enthusiasm.
75. Small businesses can be light on their feet, responding to the market and making changes quickly. More cost-efficient than their competition, they can charge less.
76. Small business adaptability permits wider selection and customized service. While it can take a large company up to five years to research and develop a product, a small company can offer a new product much more quickly.

CHAPTER 15

Sweat Equity

An entrepreneur invests not only money, but also time in a business. We call this sweat equity. Working long, hard hours while not taking cash out of the business builds a future for you and your company. It is not unreasonable to expect to work for one year before taking a salary. Of course, you may need to pull some capital out of your business, but only what you absolutely need to survive.

Typically, the owner will not receive a significant return on sweat equity until the company is either sold, franchised or made public. The owner may make a good living, but should keep most of the profits in the business for growth. Sweat equity is an investment in your company's future, so don't expect immediate compensation.

Sweat equity, while important and fulfilling to your company, can be stressful to both the entrepreneur and his or her spouse for the first couple of years. You must be willing to work long hours and think long-term, because there are no short-term benefits. This continues for two years or more, seven days a week. Even if you take a weekend off, your mind wanders back to your business. If you're not willing to sacrifice, don't go into business for yourself.

Allow employees to earn sweat equity

Don't expect your employees to work as hard as you or to care as much as you do, because they don't own the business! But if you allow them to earn sweat equity, they will work harder. If your company is private, compensate your employees for their sweat equity by offering them profit-sharing. If your company is public, give them stock options. You may also offer small equity options to your top managers, so that when you sell the company, they'll get their fair share.

Allow your employees, regardless of their level of employment, to earn sweat equity for their hard work. If it's impossible for an employee to share in your success, how can you expect motivation and dedication? A company is only as good as its employees, and they put more oomph into it when you share the good times as well as the bad. When the company has a profitable quarter or year, share some of the wealth with your employees. Don't be greedy—share a little. A $500 bonus given to a receptionist or a sales clerk can mean more than you think. Show your employees you appreciate their hard work and long hours at the office by discussing with them and perhaps even offering career advancement. Later, when things are bad and you can't afford to give out bonuses, but you need them to go the extra mile, they'll be willing. If you don't share with them during the good times, don't expect them to share the burden in the bad times.

My own sweat equity

Many times when I first started, I personally worked 65- and 70-hour work weeks, while my 9-to-5 employees made more money than I did. I always paid my employees and the bills before taking out any money for myself. While I worked harder than anyone else, my sweat equity was an investment for myself—in my company's future. And, I never expected too much from my employees who just wanted a 40-hour work week. When I took a salary or gave bonuses to my employees, the capital came out of profits, not cash flow. A small business owner would be wise not to take a big salary from the company unless it is from profits.

How sweat equity built Subway

Fred DeLuca, co-founder of Subway, an 8,000-plus restaurant chain, started his business as an undergraduate at the University of Bridgeport in Connecticut. Struggling to make ends meet, the young student looked for a job unsuccessfully until a family friend, Pete Buck, Ph.D., came up with an idea.

"Pete had visited a restaurant in Maine that featured Italian submarine sandwiches," DeLuca explains. "'He never forgot how much he enjoyed those subs. He searched but could not find a restaurant in Connecticut that offered submarine sandwiches as delicious.

"One day, he called me with an idea," DeLuca says, "He thought we should open our own restaurant offering subs like the the ones he enjoyed in Maine.

"I was very happy to have this opportunity," he says. "Pete offered $1,000 to start the enterprise if I would contribute sweat equity. I agreed."

In 1965 DeLuca and Buck opened their first restaurant near the Bridgeport campus.

"I worked whenever I wasn't in class," DeLuca recalls, "for 10 cents above the minimum wage, $1.35 an hour. I kept $13 each week to cover living expenses and applied the balance toward my tuition. All the money I earned from working overtime was put back into the business to match Pete's investment.

"I was very happy with this arrangement. I made enough money to pay for my education," he exclaims, "and I owned my own business!"

DeLuca believes the sweat equity he put into his business paid off immediately because he had the opportunity to work toward an objective—owning a business.

"The business didn't make a profit until our fourth year in business," the entrepreneur recalls. "But the sweat equity I put into the business was really worth it!"

REMEMBER

77. Every new business requires a tremendous amount of sweat equity from its owner, but typically the owner will not receive a significant return until the company is sold, franchised or made public.
78. Allow your employees to earn sweat equity for their hard work, regardless of their level of employment.
79. Your salary and bonuses given to employees should come out of your business's profits, and not from the cash flow.

CHAPTER 16

Nothing Happens Until Something Is Sold

Your company may have the best product in the world and the greatest marketing and advertising campaign, but without a sale, you will not be in business for long. You need to sell a product or a service to a customer to be in business—money must change hands, or you will not survive.

Selling is a fundamental aspect of every business, regardless of the product or service. The wide spectrum of businesses, from law firms to refrigerator manufacturers, must sell to stay in business. For example, attorneys sell their services, for without a client, there is no work to be done. In order for a company to survive, it must sell its goods.

Being an entrepreneur is synonymous with being a salesperson. If you do not have sales and marketing experience, this is one of the few good reasons why you should consider entering into a partnership.

Selling yourself and your business

Be confident! To sell, you must first sell yourself. To do this successfully requires self-confidence. The more assured you are, the easier it is for others to trust and rely upon you. If you lack self-confidence, you'll have a difficult time convincing others to buy from you.

Selling begins when you begin to seek start-up capital. This is the time to sell yourself and your business to potential investors or lenders. For example, you attempt to convince a banker to give you a loan. If the bankers have no confidence in you, there is little chance they will guarantee a loan of any size. At a time when your business is nothing more than a concept on a piece of paper, the sales job of your life is to convince others to believe in your dream.

After you secure financing to start your business, it is time to sell your business to your suppliers and manufacturers. You need to gain their trust so they will help you develop your products. If they don't believe in you, they will not extend you the credit that you need.

Another sales job will be to sell your employees. If your employees don't believe in you, they won't see a future in working for your company. Again, you want your people to think long-term. Employees must believe in their leader, the business they work for and the products or services they sell.

Employees need to trust you or they'll doubt every decision you make. It's critical that everybody involved in your business trusts your judgment and that your business is a viable, economical, good business to be a part of. If they feel otherwise, they can't possibly do their jobs well. If this is the case, these employees shouldn't be working for your company. Your employees need to be your greatest supporters, so they can represent your business effectively. If employees don't believe in what your company does, how can you expect them to sell your products or services to a customer?

You sell yourself to your customers.
You sell yourself to your spouse.
You sell yourself to your children.
You sell yourself to your employees.
You sell yourself to your banker.
You sell yourself to your suppliers.
You sell yourself to everyone!

REMEMBER

80. Your company may have the best product or the greatest marketing and advertising campaign in the world, but without a sale, you will not be in business for long.
81. Selling is a fundamental aspect of every business, regardless of the product or service you offer.
82. Be confident! In order to sell, you must be capable of selling yourself. To do this successfully requires a great deal of self-confidence. If you lack self-confidence, you'll have a very difficult time convincing others they should buy from you.
83. Selling begins when you are in the process of seeking start-up capital—you will need to sell yourself and your business to potential investors or lenders.
84. You will need to sell your business to your suppliers and manufacturers and gain their trust so they will help you develop your products.
85. You must sell yourself to your employees—if your employees don't believe in you, they won't believe in what they do or are capable of performing.
86. Employees must believe in their leader, the business they work for, and the products or services it sells.

CHAPTER 17

Dealing With Rejection

Rejection and fear of it are big barriers along the road to success. You'll be faced with rejection in every stage of your business. But that's what business is all about. Many times you'll work from sunrise to sunset until you're ready to collapse—without a single sale. It is very discouraging to work hard only to be rejected by the market. Rejection is the single most common reason business owners give up. Don't let rejection do this to you. Use your rejection as motivation to get the job done.

Accepting and learning from "no's"

Accepting "no" is part of the process you must endure as the owner of a business. Sorry to say, you will hear "no" more frequently than you will hear "yes." Learn from the rejection by asking yourself the following questions: Does my product fulfill my customer's needs? Is my price too high? Is my customer service good enough? There is much to learn from rejection.

The need for thick skin

Many people run at the first sign of adversity. They start a business and when things don't go right, they give up and go on to something else. You must be tough enough not to take the rejection to heart. Don't be sensitive every time things don't go your way. Draw upon your self-confidence. You need to be thick-skinned so you won't give up. If you know your company is doing its best by providing good service and products, don't let rejection intimidate you. Be resilient and handle the rejection in a professional manner.

I faced my share of rejection trying to sell my first few franchises. People turned me down flat. I had a difficult time convincing them my company offered wonderful opportunities. Yet I never accepted a no as a final decision—it was a definite maybe! I have turned many no's into yes's by telling the customer, "I hear your answer, but maybe we can do business together in the future. I'll keep in touch."

So I kept them on the mailing list and every month I updated them on every franchise I sold and how each was doing. Many of the people who rejected me changed their minds! They did this because I didn't let them forget about me. Out of sight, out of mind!

Persevere to stick to your plan. Don't let nasty old rejection stand in your way. No business succeeds overnight—if your concept has a realistic market potential and you are completely committed to your business, you will, I repeat, you will find success.

Dunkin' Donuts

Bill Rosenberg, founder of Dunkin' Donuts faced his share of rejection when he decided to franchise his doughnut shop. He went to his bank with full confidence that he would secure the necessary financing to begin a successful franchise business.

"Only coffee and doughnuts? Why would you want to carry only two products? Why don't you add soup and sandwiches? It simply won't work," he was told.

"You may be right," Rosenberg retorted. "But look at the Coca-Cola Company. It only has one product, and it's a refreshment. Coffee and doughnuts are breakfast items, desserts, picnic items, *and* refreshments."

But bankers considered Rosenberg a poor risk. He was turned down by his bank and every other one he went to.

It wasn't until the entrepreneur was able to assemble a group of investors that he was able to finance the franchising of new stores. He sold his first franchise in 1955 and, within eight years, 100 stores were doing $10 million in sales. Dunkin' Donuts currently has more than 3,000 stores worldwide, including locations in Saudi Arabia, Indonesia, Thailand, Korea, Singapore, Europe, Brazil, the United Kingdom and Japan, with system-wide sales in excess of $1.2 billion. If Bill Rosenberg had listened to those stodgy bankers, and let their rejection keep him from pursuing his dream, Dunkin' Donuts would not be found in every corner of the globe today.

REMEMBER

87. Rejection and fear of it are the big barriers on the road to success. Prepare to face rejection—in every stage of your business.
88. Learn from rejection by asking yourself the following questions: Does your product fulfill your customer's needs? Is your price too high? Is your service excellent?
89. Never accept no as a final decision—it is a definite maybe!
90. Be tough—and don't give up!

CHAPTER 18

Headaches I Never Dreamed Would Happen

Every entrepreneur has headaches along the way. Usually caused by problems or obstacles, these headaches are never imagined by the entrepreneur until they actually happen. After starting my own business, I experienced my own share.

My headaches began when reality fell short of my expectations. For example, often we didn't meet our sales goals and our expenses were always higher than expected. I know now that everything, beginning with product development, takes longer and costs more than expected. Some headaches stemmed from the constant disappointment I faced with many of my associates, from employees to suppliers and customers. I came to these realizations only after enduring hundreds of sleepless nights.

Headaches caused by employees

Nobody has ever hired a bad employee—or at least they don't admit it. You never know what you are going to get when you hire someone. I've been burned, and so has every other business owner at one time or another. Of course, no one ever hires a bad employee on purpose, but somehow we all get stuck with them. I had my share of bad employees because I was convinced I had found the right person based only on a resume and interview. Unfortunately, you never know *exactly* the type of employee this person is going to be until after you have already hired him or her. Hiring is a terrific gamble because, quite frankly, you just can't rely on references from previous employers anymore—they won't tell you what you need to hear because they fear a lawsuit.

Once you have hired, it doesn't get any easier. The employee relationship involves complicated issues. After all, it is a lot easier to hire than it is to fire! If your employee isn't working out, and you want to let him or her go, you have to worry about a wrongful termination lawsuit. Your terminated employee may even go to work for your competition! I was always amazed to discover how many competitors had contacted my best employees and tried to lure them away. I had my share of employees who didn't get along with each other—they fought like cats and dogs. I never before realized what a headache it can be when your employees have personality conflicts.

I was once bitterly disappointed when I caught one of my employees stealing red-handed from my business. I chose not to prosecute, but I did fire him. You can imagine my shock and dismay when this same employee sued me for wrongful termination! We ended up settling out of court. I was amazed this could happen. It was something I never expected, and it reminded me of the story of the robber who fell through the roof while breaking into a victim's home. He broke both his legs and sued the homeowner for compensation!

Another headache you have to worry about is when an employee calls in sick or is away on a vacation. Someone—perhaps even you—will have to fill in for that person. I can recall many times when my own employees failed to show up for work and I had to rearrange my whole day or week so I could do the job for them. This is all part of owning a business!

Another headache that people don't anticipate when they go into business is the high cost of employees. Not only do you have to figure a salary into your budget, but there's probably a benefits package—which can be expensive. You'll have to consider additional costs and concerns such as health insurance, Social Security and FICA taxes, a

401K program, pension plan, maternity leave, vacation and sick days. For some, these benefits can cost up to 30 percent or more of the employee's salary.

Headaches caused by suppliers and customers

I have been disappointed more than once by suppliers and manufacturers who promised deliveries on a specific date and were late. Of course, they expected to be paid in a timely manner, but didn't always fulfill their obligation to treat me with the same respect.

Customers are a different story. Some customers have become more than just customers—they've become good friends—while others tried to manipulate my business. They expected goods or service on time, but didn't hesitate to pay late!

I know the philosophy well—the customer is always right. Yet some won't hesitate to tell you they've been overcharged for a service. On the other hand, if the mistake were in their favor, do you think they will say, "I was undercharged!"? If you want to keep every customer, you will have to try your best to please them, even if it gives you a headache!

Operating on a shoestring

Most people have no concept of what it is like to run a business. My own friends and family sometimes failed to extend compassion to me after I was up all night worrying about not making payroll! I know many entrepreneurs who experienced these same struggles—not being able to pay bills on time. This is not unusual and it happens to nearly everybody who owns a business—most young businesses are undercapitalized and frequently have money crunches.

Lord knows I had cash flow problems! I remember writing checks on Thursday against an empty bank account, then nervously calling on and collecting from outstanding accounts the next day so my checks would clear. When every penny counts and you find yourself on a shoestring budget, you have to be creative to avoid the many headaches that can occur at these times.

How can you be creative? If you are cash poor, one thing you can do is avoid buying too much inventory—buy it as it is needed. Though it may be more expensive to do it this way, it'll help keep your overhead down. Spend conservatively to avoid some of these headaches down the road.

Unpaid debts

Most businesses at one time or another have their share of unpaid debts that are owed them. Collecting these debts can be costly and time-consuming. If the debt is small, don't pursue a lawsuit. Instead, go to small claims court. Even if the debt is slightly larger than the limit established at your small claims court, it may be more economical for you to go after the maximum allowed rather than the entire amount. These small debts can add up. Small claims court is an inexpensive way to collect overdue accounts.

Problem-solving

Owning a business requires constant problem-solving. Every day when I go to my office, I am never disappointed—there is always some problem for me to deal with and solve! As the owner of a business, you can prepare for headaches that come with the territory!

The best advice I can offer to a new business owner is this: Before it is too late, deal with your problems by investigating what needs to get done. If you're prepared for your headaches, they won't turn into migraines!

No bad surprises, only good ones

You probably realize what a headache it can be when you know your company cannot deliver what is expected to a business associate, financier or customer—whether it be quarterly projections, a payment or new product. My advice is this: Plant the seed early, so you will avoid the headaches later.

When my company had a bad quarter—for example, when a certain projection was not going to be achieved and I was certain by the middle of the quarter, we would come up short, I didn't hesitate to call my banker to let him know. I explained, "Our business has been a little soft. We are still hoping for the best, but we really don't think we are going to make our first quarter projection." I made sure my banker understood the problem so he would be prepared for the disappointing quarterly review statement to come.

Like every company does at one time or another, I owed my vendors money. The day the money I didn't have was due, I always called and said, "I know I owe you money, but business is tight right now, so it will be two more weeks before I can pay." If you are upfront and tell people what the situation is rather than avoid it, they will probably understand. This is much better than letting them worry about why they have not been paid on time. If they are not aware of your plans, they may conclude they are not going to be paid at all. Suppliers don't like being in the position of having to call a customer and ask for money. Deliver bad news as early as possible, to avoid giving unpleasant surprises down the road.

Another entrepreneur's headaches

Doug Mellinger, Chairman and CEO of PRT Corp. of America, a computer software development, re-engineering and forward engineering company, in New York has had his share of headaches along the road to success.

"One my biggest headaches was with accounts receivable," recalls Mellinger. "I never dreamed I would have such problems! When money was not paid on time, we were overdue with our own bills. The banks were not always understanding, especially when the accounts receivable amount doubled from one month to the next.

"I don't think many entrepreneurs think about the many organizational, financial and legal issues they'll have to face," says Mellinger.

"Personally, I never realized I would have to spend so much time with lawyers and bankers.

"I experienced another headache when a former employee left to start a competing company," recalls the entrepreneur. "This was something I had not anticipated and I was surprised and upset, but there wasn't much I could do to prevent it."

Mellinger believes that entrepreneurs start out with a pie-in-the-sky attitude. "They are not ready for the bricks that hit them in the head every day," he tells.

The entrepreneur credits his mentors with preparation he needed for the headaches he faced and still faces. "My mentors warned me what to expect. When I did have problems, they were always available for advice."

REMEMBER

91. You will face disappointments with many of your associates—from employees to suppliers and customers.
92. Cross train your employees so when one calls in sick or is away on a vacation, you'll be prepared, having someone ready to fill in for that person.
93. Suppliers and manufacturers will sometimes be late.
94. Customers expect goods or services on time, but don't hesitate to pay late.
95. You may not be able to pay bills on time. Since most young businesses are undercapitalized, this is not unusual and it happens to nearly everybody who owns a business.
96. As a last resort, small claims court is an inexpensive way to collect overdue accounts.
97. Before it is too late, deal with problems by doing investigative work; figure out what needs to get done.

CHAPTER 19

Owning A Business Is Not All It's Cracked Up to Be

What a tremendous gap there is between the perception and reality of owning a business! Aspiring entrepreneurs have to make many choices in life in order to achieve success. No one can make them successful except themselves. Entrepreneur "wanna-be's" talk the talk, but will they walk the walk? They say, "Sure, I want to be an entrepreneur. I'll work as hard as I can and do anything I have to do to achieve success." And they do—for three or four months. All of a sudden, when the work is no longer novel, it's back to playing tennis or golf every weekend. People often ask me, "Do I have what it takes?" I reply, "Would you stay up all Thursday night to make Friday's payroll?"

Taking the first step

The most difficult part of starting a business is just getting the nerve to take the first step. It's just fear that prevents people from trying. The older you are the more difficult it can be. If you have a mortgage, car payments, children and a spouse to support, you may have so many responsibilities you're not willing to take the necessary risk. No matter what business you start, there are risks.

Minimize these risks by doing your homework before diving in. Leave those unrealistic expectations behind! Some folks buy a business just to find out they don't really enjoy it day-in and day-out. Do your research first! Interview people in the same business, or try working for someone else on weekends to see if you enjoy what that business is all about.

People who start a business with unrealistic expectations are setting themselves up for failure. Don't get me wrong—owning a business is very fulfilling and rewarding, but some people go into it with idealistic expectations. Do you think you can hire people to do the work while you sit back and watch? Sorry, Charlie, it just doesn't work that way. It's hard not to be discouraged when you work very hard and might not make any money the first year. Some folks get thoroughly discouraged during this first year in business as their lifestyle diminishes and the long, hard hours increase. Didn't your grandmother tell you, you must be willing to take a step backward to go forward? No business guarantees success, but you can *increase* your odds! Don't give up—it's worth every sacrifice.

It's lonely at the top

Your time card-punching friends may think that because you own a business, you make a lot of money, and since you're the boss, you've got nothing to worry about. Try as you might to explain it to them, few will understand.

A curious thing about starting a business is your whole life changes, yet those around you have no compassion about what you're going through. Clueless as they are, no matter what you tell them, they won't understand! And if there are problems, you sure can't talk to your buddies anymore. You hesitate to dwell on your problems around your spouse because it makes him or her nervous. You can't turn to employees because they may lose confidence in you and begin to look around for another job. Very few people can relate to your trials as a business owner.

This is why it is a good idea to join a support group. For example, I became involved with Young Entrepreneurs Organization. They provided me with an outlet and the ability to meet other people who understood what I was going through. There are tens of thousands of other associations out there—representing every industry in existence. Getting the most out of an association involves more than just getting the literature and attending some of the meetings. If you become actively involved with your industry group, you'll meet dozens of other entrepreneurs who are experiencing the same issues as you.

And thank goodness for your mentor! You will need someone to talk to. Nothing's worse than feeling like you are out there by yourself.

You made the right choice—you're doing it!

Exactly how much money do you want to make? And just how hard are you willing to work for it? Initially, your business needs to break even. Later, your profit makes it possible to achieve your goals. Go into business with realistic expectations. Not every entrepreneur makes millions of dollars.

In your business's infancy, you may work out of your home to avoid an expensive office. The long, tedious hours hold pressures, a payroll to meet and a drawer full of bills—often without cash flow to cover them. To meet these expenses, you might not be able to draw your paycheck for the week. It's a shock to discover that your employees take home more money than you do.

An average small business may see up to 24 months before turning a profit. Few entrepreneurs make money their first year. If they do take a salary, the money often comes from cash flow. Many entrepreneurs fail because they overspend. They never go out of business for underspending. The sweat equity you put into the company will build a future for yourself. Use this knowledge to keep you going!

Personal sacrifices

Are you willing to give up going to your son's Little League games or seeing your daughter at her gymnastic recital? Are you willing to miss dinners with the family, and Saturday and Sunday afternoons at the golf course? A tremendous amount of guilt comes with the territory. For a company to survive and support a family, an entrepreneur must commit at least five years of long hours. You won't spend as much time with your family. You'll feel responsibility on your shoulders at all times and you will never stop thinking about your business—even on vacation.

Owning a business is a very difficult journey and if you're not willing to make the necessary sacrifices or if your family is not supportive, then don't do it! Your spouse needs to be supportive of your business and understand when you aren't home for dinner at 5:00 p.m. Many people believe they can make the necessary sacrifices for their business, but don't realize how difficult it will be. They wrongly believe that owning a business is going to be easy—it is not! The hardest part is there's always a chance your business will fail, even with all your hard work, investment and commitment. This risk every entrepreneur takes. But as the saying goes, nobody ever promised you a rose garden.

REMEMBER

98. You made the right choice—you're doing it!
99. Entrepreneurs who aspire to success, have chosen to sacrifice.
100. Many entrepreneurs fail because they overspend. They never go out of business for underspending.
101. Be willing to take a step backward if you want to go forward. No business guarantees success.
102. Decide how much money you want and how hard you are willing to work for it.
103. Most people give up because they can't take rejection.
104. Join a support group such as Young Entrepreneurs Organization, Young Presidents Organization or an association affiliated with your company's industry. The people you meet through these organizations will understand your difficulties and give you advice and support.

CHAPTER 20

Don't Count On Friends or Relatives

As a new business owner, don't be surprised if the friends and relatives you hoped would be your first customers let you down. In the beginning, they're your toughest critics. Why? They think of you as their friend, tennis buddy or lunch partner. Very few of them have business confidence in you. You might feel the same way if the heart surgeon who was about to perform your triple bypass turned out to be your former paperboy!

This discriminating group expects you to prove yourself before they'll do business with you. Most entrepreneurs have friends and relatives who promised to be their first customers. We all heard the same things: "I'll be your first customer," your brother may have said. "We'll always buy from you," your lunch buddies probably assured you. But when push comes to shove, don't build business plans around what could be empty promises.

If you're fortunate enough to have 50 acquaintances who use your services, it could mean trouble down the line. Those who have an easy time selling their first customers, can find dealing with the rest of the public a different ball game. A new business owner may feel discouraged, saying "But it was so easy in the beginning!" If you do count on friends and relatives for business, you may have set unrealistic expectations for yourself.

It's only a matter of time before you exhaust your supply of friends and relatives. So, even if you have 100 acquaintances, remember, there are 250 million people in this country. Better to go after the majority than spend time with the 100 "easy" sales. You'll gain a realistic view of the business climate much sooner.

The jealousy factor

While a few of your friends offer you moral support, many will be just plain jealous. People around you who don't own their own businesses will envy your accomplishments. I contend that most people hate their jobs. Don't depend on moral support from your friends and relatives. Simply put, they resent that you're your own boss (you should only make the money they *think* you do!). I hate to tell you how common jealousy is among the friends and families of start-up entrepreneurs. People who hate their jobs may not take pleasure in the joy that you get from yours.

My family discount is retail plus tax!

I was disappointed when some of my friends and relatives didn't follow through after promising to use my company—and if they did come through, they were often the toughest customers. And, if something goes wrong with your company's product or service, you may risk losing a close friend. Friends and relatives not only expect a discount, they want priority treatment! And, get this, they may be secretly insulted if you profit from them. You'll get some of that kind of business, but do you really need it? My family discount is retail plus tax!

REMEMBER

105. Don't build your business plan just around friends and relatives. Counting on friends and relatives as the main source for business is unrealistic.
106. People around you who don't own their own businesses envy your accomplishments.
107. Friends and relatives are sometimes the hardest customers to satisfy. Not only do they expect a discount, but they want priority treatment.

CHAPTER 21

Networking

Networking is crucial for every entrepreneur. You will be amazed to discover how it can help your business when you least expect it! You can never over-network. You have nothing to lose and everything to gain. Networking offers many opportunities—through it, you meet experienced business owners, discover new ideas and learn innovative ways to do business. Many people wrongly believe they must pay for advice for it to be worthwhile. You can never receive enough advice, paid or free! It's amazing how many people whom you would never expect to help you, can. You'll never know until you let them!

There are many places to network

You have countless opportunities to network, no matter what business you're in. Structured organizations that provide opportunities to network exist in virtually every community. For example, your local chamber of commerce may be the best place to start. Every chamber of commerce has the same purpose: to promote business within its community. Your business can join, regardless of its size. Once a member, you can network with other members. The chamber of commerce can be a valuable source of new business contacts and leads. Furthermore, you can keep up-to-date with your community—learning information about marketing trends and even sales tips. This is especially valuable for home-based businesses isolated from the business community. It is worthwhile to know as many people as possible and get your name out there.

You are not limited to networking at structured settings such as rotary or chamber meetings. Meeting people in a social setting is even better. In fact, the more informal the networking setting is, the more people let their guard down. It is easier to strike a deal with someone at a cocktail party, than at the office.

I initiated a lot of business when networking at social gatherings. For example, I had tried unsuccessfully to do business with a large builder in Los Angeles for several years. His secretary would never forward my messages to him, and he never returned my calls. By pure coincidence, he was seated next to me at a wedding reception! I was surprised to discover how friendly he was. He was fascinated when I told him about my closet business and asked me to give him a call. As it turned out, he ended up giving me plenty of business. For two years, I had tried in vain to sell my concept to him, but never had the chance until I met him at a social gathering. You try it, and see what happens!

Associations and organizations

There are thousands of associations to join representing every industry and interest under the sun. As a member of any organization, you will meet all types of people—some of whom may be able to help your business.

Joining the Rotary Club, Lion's Club and even volunteering for a charity such as the March of Dimes or the American Cancer Society are excellent ways to network within your local business community.

You may also choose to join one of the many national entrepreneurial groups around. As a member, you'll meet people who have experiences similar to yours, who can provide support and advice you need.

If you franchise your business, you will be eligible to join the International Franchising Association. Through my active membership with the IFA, I became acquainted with many company founders who also franchised their businesses. They taught me valuable information about franchising, which was tremendously helpful in developing my business.

Any association you join will be very helpful. When you become a member, make a great effort to become acquainted with as many people as possible in your industry or related fields. They can give you valuable leads, and tell others about your business.

How networking changed my life

One evening, when I was 21, I was at a friend's house for a small party. I had to leave early because I had an appointment the next morning. When my friend asked who the appointment was with, I explained I had a brochure that needed to be printed and I was meeting with a printer. Someone overheard our conversation and said, "I work for a great printing company. Why don't you let us do the job for you?" Handing me his card, he said, "Call my boss and make an appointment to come in!"

The next morning I made the appointment. When I went in, I met his boss, Michael LeVine, whose father, Bill, founded PIP printing. I was very impressed with LeVine's operation so I gave the job to the company.

A week later, Michael called me and told me he wanted to introduce me to his father. He took me to his father's office and we hit it off. At the time, I had no idea this man would become one of the biggest influences in the development of my business and my career. Bill LeVine not only created the quick-print business, but also a company that had more than 1,100 franchises. Bill took me under his wing and gave me more great advice than I can ever thank him for.

I learned how quickly things can change through networking. Because I had mentioned my appointment with a printer, I met Bill LeVine. Bill eventually joined my board of directors and became like a second father to me.

Networking works!

Doug Mellinger, president and CEO of PRT Corp. of America, a New York-based company that specializes in the planning, implementation and knowledge transfer of advanced computer technology, has used networking to his advantage over the years. Mellinger started networking while a college student at Syracuse University in New York. There, the aspiring businessman became involved with the Association of Collegiate Entrepreneurs and the local chamber of commerce. Now, he is an active member of Young Entrepreneurs Organization amongst countless other associations.

"I realized early on that to get things done quickly, you have to know people," he recalls. "I understood the benefits of networking and am certain I wouldn't be where I am today were it not for the networking.

Mellinger says that an entrepreneur should target the people he or she wants to become acquainted with. "Identify who you want to meet and find a way to get to them," he explains. "I networked my way to top people. I chose to network first with a company's CEO or CIO, and then worked my way down to other upper management."

Finding organizations to become active with is the first step. Mellinger found his by going to the library and looking through the *Encyclopedia of Associations*—a networker's dream. This book lists tens of thousands of associations in the United States and categorizes them by type. Every association imaginable representing a wide range of avocations and occupations is in this encyclopedia.

Mellinger became active with several associations and found each to be useful in growing his business.

"I am so surprised that more people don't take advantage of all the associations in their industry," he exclaims. "But, being a member of an association is more than just receiving the literature or attending some of the meetings. You need to get to know the membership—the players in your industry."

"When you attend your association's meetings, you have to ask people a lot of questions and get their business cards," Mellinger tells. "I am not afraid to approach people, introduce myself, ask them about their businesses, and get their business cards. As soon as I get home, I write on the back of each business card where I met the person and what we discussed. Then, I use the business cards to create a data base of people I can call on in the future."

"If you fail to network and let people know who you are, you will be the real loser," he continues. "I make myself very well-known. I believe the more I am out there, the more contacts I make and the more people get to know me."

"Being too busy to network is no excuse," he adds. "If you don't find out what is going on outside of your organization, you will miss out on a lot of opportunities. Networking is a very simple thing, and it is amazing how so many people don't do it."

Mellinger attributes his networking to be partially responsible for the success his business has enjoyed since its inception. In four short years, PRT's sales have grown over 1,800 percent!

REMEMBER

108. Networking is crucial for every entrepreneur.
109. Networking offers many opportunities—you will meet experienced people, discover new ideas and learn innovative ways to do business.
110. There are many opportunities to network, no matter what business you are in. Start with your local chamber of commerce, rotary club, trade associations and entrepreneurial organizations.

CHAPTER 22

The Specialist

In today's fiercely competitive marketplace, the specialist has a distinctive edge. You only have to look at the professions to realize today is the age of the specialist. In the field of medicine, physicians specialize in virtually every part of the human anatomy ranging from the foot to the brain. Specialties include such practices as internal medicine, plastic surgery, heart and thoracic surgery, and ophthalmology. The list goes on and on.

Attorneys also specialize. Their array of legal areas includes business law, malpractice, probate, personal injury, criminal defense, domestic relations and worker's compensation. Within specialties, there are still more specialists. In business law, for example, practices exist in limited areas such as bankruptcy, collections, corporate law, labor, real estate, securities and many more. The one-man law firm with the sign reading "General Law" is becoming a thing of the past, for good reason. The legal profession is far too complicated for an individual to be well-versed in all aspects.

Likewise, architects, accountants, contractors and engineers have their own areas of specialties. As the world gets smaller, it appears that areas of expertise shrink. And, it also seems that the more individuals specialize, the higher the fees they charge.

Practice makes perfect

Let's be practical. It's a lot easier to excel in one area than at everything at once. I realized long ago I didn't have the brain power of an Einstein. But many businesspeople act as if they do. They attempt to be best at all things, but end up being mediocre at everything. It takes all the effort one can muster to be exceptional at a single endeavor. The more you undertake, the thinner you spread yourself. Eventually, you are no better than the rest of the pack.

An Olympic athlete doesn't compete in swimming, track and volleyball. It's hard enough to be a world-class athlete in one event, let alone events in other fields. Why? Because practice makes perfect. To compete at this high level takes day-and-night commitment to become the best. If you become a student in your one area of expertise, chances are you'll be exceptional at what you do.

Staying focused

Typically, getting new business is a constant struggle for the start-up entrepreneur. After you hang out your open-for-business sign, the world still may not beat a path to your door. If you work long, hard hours to scratch out a living, you may be tempted to take any business that comes your way.

At 17, I was too naive to understand the principle of being a specialist. So I guess I lucked out when I made the decision to specialize in remodeling closets. Only later did I realize how smart I was to concentrate on a single area—the room considered least important in the house.

Because it was viewed with such little importance, nobody had ever made it a specialty. Consequently, I didn't have scores of competitors. If so, I would have had a difficult time making ends meet. After all, I wasn't exactly what you'd call a highly skilled carpenter, and even if I was, there were already hundreds of them in the Los Angeles area in what appeared to be an over-crowded field. Had I solicited homeowners and apartment dwellers for their general carpentry work—going after remodeling jobs such as kitchen cabinets, bookshelves and odds-and-ends fix-ups, I would have been just another carpenter trying to survive the rat race.

I, too, was frequently tempted to take on unrelated work, work that had nothing to do with closets. After installing a beautiful, well-organized closet, it was not uncommon for a customer to say: "You did such a wonderful job on that, now we'd like you to remodel our kitchen."

"I only do closets," I'd reply. "But I'll be happy to recommend somebody to you for your carpentry work."

"But we want you, Neil."

They couldn't seem to understand why I'd pass up a job much bigger than remodeling their closet. Well-intentioned friends would advise me: "Once your foot is in the door, and you win over a customer's confidence, you will be a fool not to take their kitchens, bathrooms, game rooms and garages. Neil, you're making a big mistake to pass up the more lucrative work."

Still others would say, "You're wearing blinders, Neil. It's as if you're walking down a road and picking up only the pennies when there are quarters, half-dollars and dollar bills on both sides of you."

I didn't give in to these temptations because, first, through referrals of satisfied customers, I was booked up for weeks in advance to do closets. Then, too, because I lacked experience, I didn't have the confidence to think I could perform these other types of jobs. I only knew that I could do a superior job on closets.

It's easy for a fledgling businessperson who begins a small enterprise to get side-tracked and venture off into another area beyond his or her specialty. For instance, a small haberdasher who specializes in fine clothing and accessories may be approached by a regular customer who says: "You ought to sell outerwear. I'm in the market for a raincoat and overcoat but since you don't carry them, I'll have to take my business elsewhere."

Thinking of the extra money he could generate, and concerned about losing a valuable customer, the haberdasher replies, "Well, I guess I could put in a special order for you."

"After all," he thinks to himself, "my customer may end up buying his suits from the guy down the street."

"No special orders for me," the customer says. "I want a selection of coats to choose from."

When still other customers make the same comment, the idea of selling outerwear becomes increasingly tempting. There will be times when you are tempted to deviate from your specialty to generate additional business. In a word: Don't.

Big or small, specialize!

The McDonald's success story is a classic example of specialization. Ray Kroc devised a specialization when he founded McDonald's. Nobody ever dared to tamper with his formula for selling hamburgers, fries, soft drinks and milk shakes. Every McDonald's unit operated like every other store in the chain—menus were identical, french fries measured the same in length, and Boston Big Macs tasted the same as San Diego Big Macs. Kroc made a religion of standardization—nothing was left to chance. The customer knew what to expect at McDonald's. "No surprises" was a formula that practically guaranteed success for every franchisee.

Many other hamburger stands opened since the 1950s; certainly, some have produced a product on par with or even better than the hamburgers McDonald's sold. I wager that thousands of these small restaurant operators changed their menus over the course of time, often on the advice of well-meaning customers and friends. "I'd come here more often, if you'd sell hot dogs and corned beef sandwiches," a bored customer suggests. "I can't eat hamburgers every day. I'd like some variety." Or, "Why don't you offer desserts?" and "You ought to sell pasta. There's a lot of profit in pasta."

Well-intentioned customers, friends and even employees offering tips on how to improve your business by changing your format, can tempt you to lose your focus. "Your problem is," they say convincingly, "you resist change. You're like an ostrich with its head in the sand. You've got to change with the times."

While I'm not opposed to progress, changing a successful formula can spell disaster for you. You must tread the thin line between making constant improvements within your area of specialization and changing it for the worse.

You can't have something for everybody

Even General Motors, the biggest industrial company in the world, came to realize it can't succeed in today's competitive world by manufacturing a car for every customer. When it attempted to do so, the auto maker experienced an alarming drop in market share. No longer can the company live by the slogan expressed in the 1920s by its famed president Alfred Sloan, "A car for every purpose, and a car for every pocket." Presently, GM is downsizing its operations and offering fewer choices in models. After losing billions of dollars in the late 1980s and early 1990s, the giant company is back in competition by offering better, but fewer, cars.

As recently as 1972, two out of three Americans shopped at Sears, at the time the world's largest retailer. That same year, the store accounted for more than 1 percent of the country's gross national product! But, Sears lost its lead to Wal-Mart and K-Mart because it attempted to provide something for everybody. Today, Sears realizes it can't attract everyone to shop in its stores. The competition is clearly different than yesteryear; consequently, management is redefining exactly which segments of the marketplace it will cater to.

A long list of the world's biggest and formerly most successful enterprises are shrinking their marketplace. Similarly, it makes good sense for you, a small business operator with limited funds, to think along the same lines. Just as our small haberdasher can't sell a full line to every customer who walks in, neither can any business attempt to offer something for everybody. Sure, it's difficult to get customers inside your store, and once they're there, ready and eager to spend, it hurts to see them leave without a sale. And it's tougher than nails for anyone in outside sales to get a foot in the door; once in front of a "live" prospect, you'd rather die than walk out without an order. But that's the way it sometimes is. Accept as part of your business that you must let a few good catches slide through your fingers.

If giants like GM and Sears have discovered they can't offer something for everyone, you shouldn't attempt to either!

The niche player

It's potential suicide for anyone starting a new business to go head-on against established giants with proven track records. An alternative for someone just starting out in a flourishing industry is to zero in on a particular niche that has considerable potential for growth.

When identifying a market niche for your product or service, ask yourself the following questions: Who will buy your product and why will they choose your product or service over that of the competitor's?

In today's marketplace, it is more advantageous to develop a niche-based product or service. "Many niches are poorly serviced," explains Jo-Anne Dressendorfer, a marketing expert and founder and CEO of IMEDIA, Inc., a marketing firm located in Morristown, New Jersey. "Offering a niche product moves you away from being a commodity and avoids a price-only based sale."

Dressendorfer believes many opportunities exist for entrepreneurs if they succeed in finding a niche-based product or service. "Ninety-nine percent of all successful entrepreneurs are in a niche-based business," she says. "They have discovered that as a specialist, they have more of an opportunity for people to listen to them and avoid price-only based sales."

Being an expert

According to Dressendorfer, "A business can grow and prosper if it can exploit the current business environment in its field and develop a formula—a secret to success."

To do this, she believes, the entrepreneur must become a specialist—be the best in the field and an expert at the industry. "If you are a specialist, you'll have the ability to outperform those who don't understand the industry—becoming indispensable to your customer," she continues. "Your specialized knowledge will show up in increased sales and greater overall margins."

"Become an expert in your industry," she explains. "There's no time or patience for middlemen or mediocrity."

Successful niche players

Many great stories of the past quarter of a century describe the success of niche players. For instance, long after McDonald's had established itself as leader of the fast-food hamburger industry, several other companies came along that were able to compete against the world's largest restaurant chain. They did this by specializing in an area different enough to offer an attractive alternative to customers.

By 1969, thousands of golden arches had popped up across the country. That same year Dave Thomas opened a small hamburger restaurant in Columbus, Ohio. His store, Wendy's, sold a similar product but the founder's idea was decidedly different. Instead of chasing after the family with a carload of kids, he used more mature decor to sell an upscale, pricey hamburger to an adult customer. It was a big country, Thomas figured, and as long as he didn't go head-on against McDonald's, there was a market for his new business. Today, there are several thousand Wendy's around the globe.

Food chain operators continue to flock to the field, but the handful that succeed on a grand scale are niche players. Each takes a small chunk away from McDonald's, but as the industry grows, there is plenty of room for the best. Pizza was a relatively unknown food in many parts of the country back in 1958 when brothers Frank and Dan Carney opened their first Pizza Hut in Wichita, Kansas. Who could have known that pizza pie would someday give the hot dog and hamburger a run for their money as America's most popular food? Had the Carneys opened a hamburger stand instead, life might have dealt them a much different hand!

There are niche players in every industry, who are thriving and prosperous. Virtually unnoticed by industry leaders, thousands across the country have filled a small niche in a large marketplace.

Cross-fertilize your specialists

Once you people your organization with specialists from respective fields, cross-fertilize them so they will understand what your other specialists do. Why is it important for everyone to know about the other guy's specialty? It helps each department support other departments.

Your shipping clerks and billing department employees must have some understanding about what the sales force does. Likewise, a salesperson must be familiar with their jobs as well as your manufacturing process to avoid overselling customers. In short, establish teamwork within your organization. Specialists in one area need to be knowledgeable about the specialists in other areas. As the president, you must consider one of your most important responsibilities that of coordinating your various departments. This is what top management is all about. Entrepreneurs who develop teamwork among their people will see their small company grow and become a large company.

REMEMBER

111. Don't try to be good at everything—be the best at something!
112. It's easier to excel in one area than at everything.
113. You will be tempted to generate additional business by deviating from your specialty. In one word: Don't.
114. Recognize the difference between constantly improving your area of specialization, and changing it for the worse.
115. In a flourishing industry, zero in on a particular niche that has considerable potential for growth.
116. When identifying a market niche for your product or service, ask yourself the following questions: Who will buy your product and why will they choose your product or service over the competitor's?
117. Be an expert in your industry and you'll be indispensable to your customer.
118. Once you people your organization with specialists from various fields, develop their understanding of what your other specialists do.
119. When you are the best at something, people remember your company.

CHAPTER 23

The Generalist

During the business's infancy, you will be a one-person operation, forced to perform any task required. With no one to delegate to, you will be a jack-of-all-trades—a generalist. As your enterprise and your responsibilities grow, you will hire employees with expertise in specific areas such as accounting, marketing, advertising, manufacturing and warehousing. Once the company is well-staffed with these specialists, your role changes to master coordinator.

And I had a hammer

In the beginning, I installed every closet myself. Once I could afford installers, I dedicated myself to selling our product. Later, I was more involved in marketing, yet whenever I felt the need to find out what was going on with the business I observed an installation or went on a sales call. I was always ready to jump back into installation or selling when necessary.

It is essential that management understands the employees' jobs. Every so often, a manager needs to do a sales call or wait on a customer. This keeps the manager in touch with the product and capable of answering a customer's questions. As your business gets bigger, you must work harder to stay in touch with every aspect.

As a generalist, you must maintain a good understanding about every area of your business. You don't have to be an expert, but you need some knowledge or you can't tell others what you want them to do. Only a strong leader with a working knowledge of each department can motivate the specialists to perform their necessary work.

Hiring a specialist to assist you with your business doesn't mean you don't have to know the basic steps of your accounting, marketing and manufacturing. Even generalists should understand what is going on in their business.

Being a generalist without losing your niche

Certainly, the great business leaders of the past were generalists, although most of them probably started out specializing. One danger a generalist faces is thinking he or she can run any business. I've observed several presidents who say, "Business is business, and a leader who understands how to manage one company can manage any business using the same principles." In theory, this sounds feasible but in the real world of business, it rarely works.

In the 1960s, when conglomerates were in vogue and giant corporations were busy acquiring other corporations, presidents thought they had the magic touch with any company—regardless of the nature of the business. Some generalists suffered bruised egos when they discovered major differences in managing companies in unfamiliar industries. One company that got into trouble was Heublein's when it temporarily acquired Kentucky Fried Chicken in the early 1970s. As a Heublein executive said, "In the wine and liquor business, it doesn't matter what the liquor store looks like. Smirnoff Vodka doesn't get blamed if the floor is dirty. And, we can control our product at the factory. We simply bought a chain of 5,000 little factories all over the world, but didn't have the experience in handling that kind of operation."

The lesson to be learned is that the generalist should remain focused on the main business that was learned from the ground floor up. While some business principles apply to every company, differences exist. The specialist's expertise is vital in determining long-term success.

REMEMBER

120. Good management understands what its people do. As your business grows, work harder at staying in touch with every aspect.
121. Once you become a generalist, continue to maintain a good understanding about every area of your business.

CHAPTER 24

The Sales-Driven Entrepreneur

Selling is the art of persuasion—influencing someone to adopt your way of thinking or motivating a person to buy your product or service. Effective selling requires that you listen to the customer's needs and wants. It's a challenge to control the presentation without losing the customer's attention.

Listening to the customer

The only way to know the needs of your customers is to listen to what they have to say. Your job is to guide customers to conclude that they need to buy your product. You do this by asking the right questions and listening to the answers.

Too many salespeople neglect to listen to their customers. What a terrible mistake! If you get through a sales presentation without any interruptions from the prospect, that's bad news—in fact, your chances of closing will probably decline. When a salesperson gives a memorized pitch that doesn't allow for interruptions from the prospect, this dominating one-way communication alienates the customer. If a customer is not permitted or encouraged to contribute to the sales process, the salesperson can never learn what the customer's needs are. He misses out on valuable clues that will help close the sale.

You may offend customers if you don't allow them to express the need for your product. Customers resent pushy salespeople, because they'd rather feel in control of their decisions. A customer who feels pressured won't buy from you, just as a matter of principle!

When you listen and react to the customer's needs and wants, you demonstrate you care about him or her. There's nothing better than a salesperson who gives undivided attention to a client during a sales presentation. You have to sincerely put the customer's interests first. When customers believe a salesperson cares about their needs, they will trust the salesperson and want to buy from him or her.

What will this do for me?

Find out as much information about the customers as possible. After you establish what their needs are, then you can tell them about the product. Explain not only the features of the product, but how the product will benefit them and fulfill their needs.

In my own sales presentation, I described to customers how my company would install double-hanging shoe shelves and sweater shelves. Then I told them the benefits. For example, they would be able to see their sweaters at eye level, find their shoes easily, and have more hanging space. When I talk to a customer, I pretend they have a big tattoo on their forehead that says "What will this do for me?" A customer is always concerned with how a product will directly affect him or her.

Another benefit, if it applies, is good value. These days, everybody wants value for their money, no matter how rich or poor they are. One of the best ways to build value in the customer's mind is to say, "This is our best-selling product." Give them sales figures, showing that many other people find value in your product. You can also compare your prices and quality to those of your competitor.

Methods of distribution

There are many different ways to distribute your product or service to your customer, but it takes time before you will know which method is most effective for your company. The best method is the one that most effectively penetrates your market and reaches your targeted customer.

If your product is a tangible one, you may choose to sell it through retail stores, mail-order sales, telemarketing, wholesalers or directly to the customer at home. Methods that are effective for service-related companies include telemarketing, direct sales and mailers.

There are two types of sales forces to choose from: direct and independent. A direct sales force only sells your product or service, is on your payroll and under your direct control. Independent sales representatives are generally paid a commission only after they have made a sale, and are a less expensive alternative to a direct sales force. The disadvantage of using independents is that your product or service may be one of many they represent and will not receive the same personal attention a direct sales would provide. A common strategy for young companies is to initially use independent sales reps and later develop a direct sales force when it is more affordable.

Once you have established a method that works well for your company—the one that develops a core customer base—protect it and avoid any conflicts of interest that may destroy it.

Finding and developing salespeople

Finding good salespeople is a difficult process. When I need salespeople, I search for long-term employees. I can tell if someone has the potential to be with me for the long-term by looking at the experience on their resumes. I consider how long they were employed at each job and why they left their jobs. Longevity is important to me, and I won't consider someone who has jumped from one company to another. After all, it takes months of training before they are even productive, which is very costly.

I learned to beware of hiring salespeople who boast because they have sold everything to everyone, they can sell anything to anyone. They are the ones who say, "I can sell ice to Eskimos!" This may not be the kind of individual you want on your payroll. Perhaps such a salesperson has never been able to keep a job selling only one product. Use such caution when dealing with anyone boasting of many past positions in different fields.

I cannot overemphasize the importance of developing a continuous sales training program for your salespeople. Creating one is well-worth the time and effort. Your salespeople need to learn a great deal about the products they sell. They should be very familiar with your corporate goals and philosophy, and trained to provide excellent customer service. Every salesperson should be an expert, capable of servicing a customer's every need and able to answer every question asked about the product. This expert salesperson will close sales swiftly.

The sales training process at my company required the salespeople to install a closet in their own homes. We gave the salespeople a do-it-yourself kit and let them design their own closet. My salespeople were more enthusiastic about the closets if they used the product every day. They could answer more customer questions from their direct experience. People who are sold on a product, will be able to sell it. If they did not believe in it, they can't sell it to anyone. Salespeople should believe in the product or service they are selling and have the integrity to sell a product that a customer really needs.

Once salespeople have been trained in the classroom, you'll have to teach them how to give a solid presentation through first-hand experience. Take your salespeople out on a sales call with you to watch your presentation. When salespeople are ready to go out on their own, give them an easy sale—perhaps a repeat customer—to give them confidence. Rejection is very discouraging, so start them off on the right foot.

The presentation

Before giving a presentation, your salespeople should learn every detail about the product or service they will be selling. They should know the product inside and out. Every customer will agree—there's nothing more agreeable than dealing with a salesperson who knows what he or she is talking about.

Once you have hired a knowledgeable sales staff, you can teach them to present the product or service to the customer. A presentation should be brief and to the point, covering important issues while allowing time for customer questions. The more complicated and drawn-out the sales presentation, the smaller your chance to close the sale. Customers prefer to soak up information in the least amount of time. The length of a presentation has nothing to do with the value of the product, so if you get the job done effectively, quickly and painlessly, your client will appreciate your respect of his or her time.

Allow your customer to participate in the presentation. If your product is a tangible one, a car, computer or fax machine, etc., demonstrate how it works, then ask the customer to try it out. An automobile salesperson wouldn't dream of selling a car to a customer without a test drive! This is often the quickest way to "hook" the customer. While or after the customer uses the product, ask a lot of questions.

My father, Jack Balter, former vice president of sales for California Closets says, "The ingredients of a good sales presentation are the following: Listen to what the customer says, and then tell the customer what he or she wants to hear. Unfortunately, most sales people don't listen and talk too much.

"There are many important things a customer will tell you if you just listen," he adds. "Involve the customer in your presentation, by asking questions then listening to the answers. I closed a lot of sales this way. How can they say no? They probably can't because they are already involved."

Thinking big

Small entrepreneurs sometimes think they are limited to going after small clients. "It's a mistake to set such restrictions," says Jo-Anne Dressendorfer, a marketing specialist. "It's a self-imposed limitation, that because your company is small you should go after only the smaller prospects. If your product is appropriate for the big fish, then go for it! Someone has to sell them, and it might as well be you. You'll expend fewer resources. It is less costly in the long run to deal with a large client than go door-to-door searching for small ones. Always concentrate on the customer providing the greatest reward.

"If you have a product that big clients will buy, sell it to them," she continues. "After all, when you go to a larger customer, you get bigger orders. You are your only limitation. The customers are the same. Once you begin to do business with one large company, it will be easier to find another. It takes so much time to run around to 50 small customers, so why not concentrate on two or three big customers?"

Another advantage of selling a "big" customer is you don't hear "I can't afford it." As Willy Sutton, the famous bank robber once said when asked why he robbed banks, "Because that's where the money is!"

Selling John Smith

Peter Thomas, founder of CENTURY 21® real estate services in Canada, has a favorite rhyme that he believes is important to remember whenever selling:

> *To sell John Smith what John Smith buys, You see John Smith through John Smith's eyes.*

"To sell to a customer, it's critical to first understand his needs," Thomas says. "If you don't see his eyes start to twinkle, stop your presentation. Furthermore, if you think the customer is going to sleep or is thinking about a baseball game, you have to wake him up by asking questions to capture his attention.

"When giving a presentation, never use technical language," he continues. "Don't throw around industry jargon that may be second nature to you but the customer won't understand. Not only will it hurt your presentation, but most people won't tell you that they don't understand what you are saying."

"Always assume that the client knows nothing about the product," says Thomas. "And if you are selling to a group, sell to the lowest common denominator in the room—the person who knows the least about the product.

"Never talk over a customer's head," he continues, "Bring the sales presentation down to the level of the customer who is buying the product."

Thomas, who employed more than 9,000 salespeople, says, "What I learned over 30 years ago is simple," he reveals. "The first thing you do is look for a customer...then do your presentation,"

"Once you have made the sale and closed, you begin to service," he continues. "Each step is vital in the selling process, and you can't continue to sell without any one. Now in my mid-50s, this is the same as it was when I was 24 years old."

A hard sale

Horizon Foods, a gourmet food distributing company based in Fairfax, Virginia, sells directly to the home consumer, offering 200 types of frozen entrees ranging from meat to seafood and other prepared products. President Steven Krane, along with three partners, bought the company and its four original locations in 1987. Currently, Horizon has 20 locations across the United States, and 300 salespeople, grossing in excess of $30 million in retail sales a year.

According to Krane, selling door-to-door is a difficult selling process. "Our salespeople cold-canvas a neighborhood to establish a client base," he says. "Over 60 percent of our business is obtained through referrals and 90 percent of our customers repeat business.

"Our salespeople are all commissioned, independent contractors who face rejection all of the time," Krane continues. "So, it takes a certain type of salesperson to do this type of sales. I have realized all of our top salespeople are generally competitive people who have clear-cut and well-defined goals. A person needs goals and a vision to be a great salesperson. He or she needs a reason to sell or it is too easy to give up. When a salesperson knows he or she needs to work hard to meet goals, he or she will have the desire to go on to the next house and not quit early. It is too easy to give up in the face of rejection unless you have goals.

"After all, rejection is inherent in any sales position," he continues. "For example, when you consider the best professional baseball hitter of all time has a career average of around .325—this means that three times out of every 10 times at bat he got a hit. Even worse, every seven times he was at bat, he didn't even get on base! Just like baseball, a salesperson must expect his or her share of failures, too. A good salesperson will be lucky to sell to three out of every 10 customers!

"When we hire for sales positions, we look for people who have high goal levels. "We also want a person who has held a position for at least two years with a former employer," he tells. "The reason is simple: in every sales career a person is going to meet with rejection. Generally, after the salesperson faces constant rejection, he or she leaves the company to move on to something else—going from job to job. We want someone who can stick it out, and not lose confidence when he or she is rejected."

REMEMBER

122. Selling is the art of persuasion—influencing someone to your way of thinking and motivating a person to buy your product or service.
123. Listen and understand the customer's needs and wants. Control the presentation, without losing the customer's attention.
124. Every salesperson should learn every detail about the product or service he or she will be selling and know the product inside and out.
125. A sales presentation should be brief and to the point, yet covering important issues and allowing time for customer questions. The more complicated and dragged-out a sales presentation is, the smaller your chance to close the sale.
126. If your product is a tangible one, involve the customer in your presentation by first demonstrating how the product works, then allowing him or her to try it out.
127. The only way to know the needs of your customer is to listen to what they have to say—these needs are the clues that will help close the sale.
128. Customers resent pushy salespeople, and like to feel they control the decision-making process. If the customer feels pressured and becomes uncomfortable, he or she won't buy from you, even if he or she wants your product or service.
129. After you explain the product's features, tell customers how the product benefits them and fulfills their needs.
130. An ongoing sales training program is essential for good salespeople.
131. Salespeople should be familiar with corporate goals and philosophy, and trained to provide excellent customer service.
132. Salespeople should believe in the product or service they are selling and have the integrity to sell a product that a customer really needs.
133. Assume the client knows nothing about your product and never talk over a customer's head.

CHAPTER 25

Don't Keep a Secret: Ask for the Order

You may have the best product and marketing plan, but if you can't close a sale, you have nothing! As a salesperson, it is your job to gently guide the prospect into a buying decision. If you listen carefully to your customer, you can recognize certain buying signals that let you know how to make the sale.

The close is the moment of truth—the big decision the customer must make, one your success depends on. There are many different ways to close a sale. If one doesn't do the trick for you, try another! It's common to make several attempts to close a sale during a presentation. When a customer says, "I would like some time to think it over," a good salesperson doesn't let go without making every attempt possible to close.

A salesperson will not be successful at closing every time, and knows, "Nobody sells 'em all." Successful salespeople don't lose self-confidence when they fail to close—they realize they have to be percentage players. The more customers they go after, the better their chances to sell. Don't lose confidence when you are unable to close a sale—try someone else!

Closing with confidence

It is necessary to have full confidence in your ability to close the sale. If you don't, after your presentation your prospect wonders why you haven't asked for the order. Hesitation is contagious. Don't catch it! If you lack confidence to close the sale, the customer will lack confidence to make the decision.

When you close the sale with confidence, you personify success, and customers prefer dealing with successful salespeople. They might say to themselves, "For some reason, this salesperson is successful—the product must be good." If they see a lack of self-confidence, it will be difficult to close—and you may lack the nerve to even attempt closing. Don't let possible rejection keep you from asking for the order. If you don't ask, you'll never know what could result.

Jack Balter, former vice president of sales for California Closets, believes a salesperson needs both self-confidence and assertiveness—key ingredients—to close a sale.

"A salesperson has to be confident and aggressive" he says. "and unfortunately, most salespeople are hesitant to be assertive. A salesperson who is not assertive when selling will not close. Since you don't want to leave the customer without an order, you have to give it your best shot. The best way to do this is by asking for the order.

"If you are rejected, don't let it affect your psyche," he adds. "I never let rejection affect me. I just go on to the next sale."

Assume the sale

You have a positive influence on the customer when you assume the sale. When you have this attitude throughout the presentation and close with confidence and conviction, the odds of closing the sale are in your favor. You should begin to assume the sale as soon as you arrange your appointment with the customer. Any person interested in meeting with you must have a need for what you have to sell. If not, he or she wouldn't have scheduled the appointment!

Assuming the sale is a simple way to close. When done in a subtle, nonoffensive way, it can be very productive. For example, with an everyday product like gasoline, attendants are trained to ask the customer, "Should I fill it up with the premium or super unleaded?" The question asked has assumed the customer wants the maximum amount of gas the car can accommodate and one of the two most expensive varieties. If the serviceperson had asked "What kind of gas and how much would you like?" The response will probably be "Give me $10 worth of regular unleaded."

Peter Thomas, founder of CENTURY 21® real estate services in Canada, with decades of selling experience, uses the assuming-the-close technique. "I won't even make the presentation unless I know a customer needs what I am selling," says Thomas. "If I prospect a customer and he qualifies, then I assume he'll buy from me. I give the presentation, confident I will close."

When assuming the sale or employing the major-minor close (discussed in the next section), never ask the customer if he or she wants to buy directly. Don't ask, "Do you want the product? Instead, you ask, "How, when and where do you want it delivered?"

The major-minor close

As a salesperson, your job is to guide the prospect, making it easy for him or her to buy your product. You can encourage the customer to make a major decision by helping you make many minor ones.

While a procrastinator has a difficult time making major decisions, it is easier for him or her to make minor ones. The major-minor close presents many minor decisions for the prospect to make—all adding up to a major one.

A car salesperson may use this selling technique by asking a series of questions requiring minor decisions. "Do you prefer the two-door or the four-door?" "What interior and exterior colors do you like best?" And "Do you prefer a cassette or a compact disc stereo?"

I used to ask my customers, "Do you like the design? Do you think it will suit your needs? Do you like the colors we offer?" After asking many minor questions that are easy for the customer to answer, the salesperson has only the price left to discuss. This is when I would ask my customer, "Well, if we can agree on the price, can we process your order today?" This is again, another minor decision for the customer to make.

Creating a sense of urgency

When a customer is on the edge of buying, but won't budge, create a sense of urgency—this can be the difference between success or failure. This is one of the oldest and most-used techniques when closing. If you find yourself in a sales situation where the customer is on the edge of buying, the sense of urgency could be the most effective way to close—the difference between success or failure.

Regardless of what you sell, you can create a sense of urgency. You can urge the customer to act immediately by convincing the customer that the product or service will not be available later. This closing method is especially successful when the customer is a procrastinator. Urging this type of customer to buy now might be your only chance to close the sale. If you don't, between now and later, the customer will probably talk himself or herself out of the purchase.

You can express a sense of urgency to the customer in many ways, but you must be truthful. For example, you can't tell a customer your prices are going up next month if they will be the same. To misrepresent is not only unprofessional, it is dishonest. Never compromise on your integrity—never, never, never! For example, when a real estate agent creates a sense of urgency he or she might tell a client "I know you want to think this over, but this house may not be available tomorrow. It's just been put on the market and will sell fast...I know of other prospective buyers who are coming over to look at the house later this afternoon."

If you want to create a sense of urgency, and need an incentive to entice a customer to buy, sometimes, offering a bonus might be just the technique to close the sale. This can be in the form of a discount or "freebie." For example, a computer salesperson might throw in free software if a customer buys a computer. California Closets sometimes gave customers a few dozen plastic hangers. Your bonus might be enough to push the customer over the edge to buy.

Asking and asking for the order

Reg Pattemore is president and general manager of Metro Ford Sales, Ltd., one of the largest Ford dealerships in Alberta, Canada. Pattemore has worked for the family-owned and operated business since he was 14.

According to Pattemore, salespeople ask for an order, as many as three times "before letting the customer walk away." "After three failed attempts, the salesperson will send in a manager who will try to find out what the customer's objection is," says Pattemore. "Of course, if the customer is antsy or feeling pressured, we let him or her go."

"This isn't high-pressure selling—it's 'higher' pressure selling. We know there are different buttons we can push to get the order.

"We tell our customers, 'There's no time like the present,' " Pattemore continues. "We'll say, 'If I can get my manager to agree on this price will you buy it today?' It's hard to pressure a customer with a product there is an abundance of, because they know they get the same product now or in six months. This why we try to create a sense of urgency—so the customer will buy now."

Relationship selling

"A salesperson should be able to close by asking probing questions and identifying and meeting the customer's needs," says Steven Krane, president of Horizon Foods, a Fairfax, Virginia-based home shopping service that sells discounted flash-frozen gourmet food in bulk to homes and offices. "A salesperson who has not listened to what the customer has said won't close. The first thing a salesperson should find out is what are the customer's needs. Only then can the salesperson match the product to meet those needs. This is relationship selling and it is the reason why my company has a very high repeat business. We match the products to our customer's needs."

"Salespeople have a bad reputation as people who should not be trusted," concedes Krane. "This is because of the ones who employ high-pressure closing techniques. So instead asking, 'What can I sell you?' my salespeople are trained to ask, 'How can I best suit your needs?' "

REMEMBER

134. You may have the best product and marketing, but if you can't close a sale, you haven't accomplished anything—for you or your customer!
135. The close is the moment of truth—the big decision the customer must make, and one that your success depends on.
136. If one closing technique doesn't work, try another! It's common to make several attempts to close a sale during a presentation with a prospective customer.
137. Have full confidence in your ability to close a sale in order to do so.
138. Don't let fear of rejection stop you from asking for the order.
139. Assume a sale as soon as you arrange an appointment with the customer.
140. When assuming the sale or employing the major-minor close, never ask the customer directly if he or she wants to buy.
141. The major-minor close presents many minor decisions for the prospect to make—all adding up to a major one.
142. Create a sense of urgency for the customer who is on the edge of buying but won't budge.
143. There are many ways to express a sense of urgency, but you must be truthful.
144. A salesperson who has not listened to what his or her customer has said won't close.
145. Find out what the customer wants, then match the product to meet the customer's needs—this is relationship selling.
146. Don't ask, 'What can I sell you?' Instead, ask 'How can I best suit your needs?'
147. A salesperson who quits after two or three no's, will never close. No doesn't necessarily mean no, it can also mean "know"—the customer may need more information before making a decision.

CHAPTER 26

Being a Customer-Driven Company

The most difficult task when operating your own business is creating and retaining a solid base of customers, the lifeblood of every business. Without them, your business can't survive. Your competition is trying to lure your customers away—it's critical that your company provide excellent service. Customers expect a certain level of service when they choose a company to do business with. Don't disappoint them! More than for any other reason, customers quit doing business with a company because of poor service. Many are even willing to pay a premium for better customer service.

Customer service is nothing more than common courtesy. Simply put, treat your customers the way you want to be treated yourself. You must understand what your customers are thinking and follow through on any promises you make them. As the business owner, create a realistic level of service for your customers to expect, and then try to exceed those expectations. If you exceed them in any way possible, you'll have happy customers.

Understanding customer needs

Customers should have an enjoyable experience doing business with your company—one they want to repeat again. Talk to several of your customers to find out how they define satisfaction with your product or service and your company. Your customers are your best critics—listen to them to learn their desires, needs and wants. Use this information to design a customer service policy that includes the qualities important to your customers. You can begin serving them even before the order is placed, and continue providing this service throughout your relationship.

Why customers don't come back

Customers who don't repeat business with a company do so for the following reasons:

1 %	death
3 %	relocation
5 %	influence of friends
9 %	price
14 %	unresolved complaints
68 %	indifferent attitude of staff

Kill your customers with service

Customer service should be a company philosophy and every person in your organization must be a customer service representative. What separates great companies from good ones is management's ability to understand the value of customer service.

The very first time a customer has contact with your company, he or she should hear a friendly greeting, never be put on hold for more than a few seconds, and have his or her call returned promptly. Many customers walking into a store are intimidated because they do not enjoy being sold to. It is your job to make customers feel comfortable with the selling experience.

There is no such thing as too much customer service. Great companies realize it is four times harder and more expensive to create a new customer than it is to keep an existing one.

The purpose of a business is to create and keep customers. How do you do this? By extending excellent customer service and never taking customers for granted. Nordstrom, the department store, for example, bends over backwards to serve its customers. Nordstrom offers an open-return policy and excellent service, and whatever else it can to satisfy its customers. This is why its customers are willing to pay a little more for their purchases than they would at other department store chains.

Some large corporations claim to treat all customers the same. They say every customer, big or small, is equally important. This is not true. Typically, large clients get more personal service than the little guys. Normally, the chairman and the top officers of the company are each assigned a handful of companies to personally serve, and their smaller clients don't get the same attention. It is a shame that too many people are actually surprised when they receive good service. It should be the other way around—good service should be expected.

The value of loyal customers and referrals

The first few years can be difficult for a new company; however, virtually 80 percent of its future sales will be the result of repeat orders and referrals from satisfied customers. Successful businesses do backbends for their customers, knowing that a lasting business must win lifetime customers. A business that fails to maintain its customer base, is destined to pound the pavement seeking new customers. The companies who don't value repeat customers and referrals are doomed to a difficult future.

Your mission, should you choose to accept it, is to create satisfied customers. A satisfied customer may tell three friends. But bad word-of-mouth spreads even faster. Studies indicate every unhappy customer tells 11 people about the bad experience. Sure, your unhappy customers tell only their side of the story. Unfortunately, even if your company is in the right, you will not be around to explain this to your unhappy customer's friends. Negative advertising can damage a company reputation if not close it down completely. On the other hand, provide more service than expected, and you have a loyal customer who won't even consider doing business with your competition. Satisfied customers, your best and cheapest source of advertising, bring you additional business through referrals. What a return on your investment!

A customer who learns about your business from an acquaintance, is presold on your company. More than likely, he or she won't even consider doing business with your competition or compare prices. Customers trust friends' judgment, which allows your company to sell at higher prices because you are not directly competing with others for the business. The advantages of receiving business through referrals are numerous—there's no competition, you get your full retail price, and the closing rate for a sale is close to 95 percent.

After only one year, I was surprised to discover that as much as 40 to 50 percent of my company's business came from referrals and repeat customers. This confirmed my belief in treating every customer well. A customer whose expectations have been exceeded, will refer you to their friends and do everything possible to help your business. If you fall short of expectations, no gimmick, program, prize or certificate will pacify a dissatisfied customer. When you do a quality job for a customer, and your business relies on referrals, don't be shy—ask the customer to recommend you to their friends. If you have done a good job, the customer will *want* to refer your company to others.

100-percent satisfaction guaranteed

L.L. Bean, founder of the outdoor clothing and equipment catalog once promised, "A happy customer comes back. From now on all our products are guaranteed to give 100 percent satisfaction in every way." This company realized a long time ago that excellent customer service is what brings customers back to do business—and this is the backbone of its success. Many other entrepreneurs have found a

100-percent satisfaction principle a competitive advantage over the competition.

Customers are always right (even if they aren't!)

You never win an argument with a customer. If you do, you'll probably lose the customer. You are not doing your company any favors when you alienate a customer, even for all the right reasons.

Don't ever ask a customer for his or her opinion unless you are prepared to fix a problem should one arise. For example, imagine yourself a customer in a restaurant. Your waitress approaches your table and asks you if you are enjoying your meal. You respond by telling her that you found the steak to be a little tough. How would you feel if she apologized but didn't take any measures to correct the situation? What she actually did was make the situation worse, because now that she knows there is a problem. If she does not now rectify it, you will be angry. What she needs to say is, "Oh, I'm very sorry. Let me bring you another steak." Or "Let me take the meal off your bill," or "I'll bring the manager over."

When a customer has a problem, your company has the opportunity to demonstrate its exceptional service. Make your customers feel comfortable enough to call you with any complaint. Warn the customer if you expect a problem and tell him or her when and how you will solve it.

Every company has problems from time to time. Customer service-oriented companies use problems to build closer ties with customers. A customer who has a complaint that is handled in a satisfactory and professional manner can become your most loyal customer.

The IBM success story

International Business Machines (IBM), founded in 1914, built its worldwide reputation based on customer service ideas and principles. IBM has successfully kept its customers "married" to its products—and developed enormous repeat customer business—all because the

141

company approaches its customers after the sale with the same interest and attention as when the prospect is courted.

IBM realized early on that they would have been out of work without customers. They also realized that there was a limit to the number of customers they could acquire. So, while they work very hard to get a new customer, they work even harder to hold on to the ones they have. IBM considers its customers to be at the top of its organizational chart and goes to great lengths to keep every customer happy.

REMEMBER

148. Successful companies have one common denominator—they value exceptional customer service.
149. There is no such thing as too much customer service.
150. Great companies realize it is four times harder and more expensive to create a new customer than it is to keep an existing one.
151. Exceed your customers' expectations and they'll be back and refer you to their friends and relatives.
152. Don't ask a customer for his or her opinion unless you are prepared to fix a problem should there be one.
153. Virtually 80 percent of a company's future sales will depend on repeat orders and referrals from satisfied customers.
154. Studies indicate every unhappy customer tells 11 people about a bad experience.
155. Satisfied customers are the best and cheapest source of advertising, bringing additional business through referrals.
156. A customer who learns about your business from an acquaintance, is presold on your company.
157. The advantages of receiving business through referrals are numerous—there's no competition, you get your full retail price, and the closing rate for a sale is close to 95 percent.
158. When you do a quality job for a customer, don't be shy—ask the customer to recommend you to their friends.
159. Be on time for every appointment, answer every call and letter promptly, no matter who it is with—a customer, distributor, manufacturer or anyone else (calendar integrity).

CHAPTER 27

The Personal Touch

Most people consider big companies insensitive, uncaring, faceless entities. One distinct advantage a small business has over a giant is the personal touch.

Customers prefer to deal with an owner or manager on a personal basis. In the case of a small owner-operated company, each customer's patronage is really important; at the end of the day, it makes a difference to the company. For this reason, the customer believes he or she will be appreciated, and everybody wants to be appreciated.

Let's face it, people resent being treated like a number. As companies grow, they tend to get bogged down with rules and procedures. The more bureaucratic they get, the more callous and uncaring they appear. Big companies with home offices in faraway places may seem unresponsive and cold. They lack warmth and what I call the personal touch.

We care

"We care" should be a slogan for every business. People want to think the company they are doing business with cares about them. So they choose to patronize small businesses where they believe they will receive personal attention.

Remember, every person and business is in the service industry no matter what its product.

Little things make a big difference

It is unlikely your company can be 100-percent better than your competition, yet there may be 100 things you can do 1-percent better. If you work on these, particularly the ones that are service-related, your company will not only survive, but succeed! Your service sets your company apart from the rest. Sometimes this makes the difference between getting the business and not getting the business.

The little things you do for people are part of the personal touch: returning customer's phone calls promptly, writing handwritten thank-you notes and following up by asking customers if they are pleased with your work. While each little piece of the personal touch puzzle doesn't seem very important, all put together they form a picture of a company that really cares for its customer.

Little touches become big successes

As California Closets expanded around the country, we tried to project an image that helped customers know we truly cared about them. I worked hard to make sure we shouldn't give the impression of being a big business. To overcome that image, I looked for little things that my people could do so customers would know how much we cared. Often, a small or subtle thing—the personal touch—often made the best impression.

For example, our service people would track through a customer's home, in the process of organizing a closet, and make a mess. After all, carpentry work can be sloppy. So one simple thing we trained them to do was to vacuum up after completing a job. This may seem insignificant, but many customers wrote us letters expressing their appreciation.

I also had a company policy whereby our managers and franchisees would call customers about a week after an installation to make sure they were satisfied with our service. We sent thank-you notes telling customers we appreciated their business. What's more, it was always a handwritten note—again, the personal touch. These touches ultimately resulted in referrals and repeat business accounting for nearly 50 percent of our total revenue. Now, who says the personal touch doesn't make a difference?

Being big, thinking small

In the '90s, even large companies try for the personal touch. Some even go so far as sending birthday cards to loyal customers.

Mary Kay Ash, founder of Mary Kay Cosmetics, believes in the importance of the personal touch. She says, "I worried about losing the personal touch when I had 1,000 employees, then I worried about it when we had 5,000 people, and 10,000 and 20,000. I'm still worrying about it now, with more than 100,000 people in our organization! I'll always be concerned about the personal touch—and do everything in my power to see we never lose it. Now that our company has grown so large, the personal touch seems even more important."

Call the Windex guy

Shelby H. Carter, Jr., past vice president of marketing at Xerox Corporation, recalls the moment he first realized the value of the personal touch. "A very small, seemingly insignificant thing influenced me when I was a customer. After our family had just moved into a new home, the first day in the house everything was in an uproar. My children poured into the family room and the television set didn't work. I got out the yellow pages and called a repairman, who came right out. After he repaired the set, he asked me to come over and look at it. I stepped over the kids and our German shepherd, and instead of handing me a bill, he took out a bottle of window spray and cleaned the glass. It impressed me to see he was proud of his work and the product he serviced. From that day on, whenever we've needed our TV fixed, I've said to my wife, 'Honey, call the Windex guy.' He's got pride in his work, and I respect him for that."

Calendar integrity

Buck Rogers, who headed IBM's worldwide marketing organization for many years, says, "I can't tolerate bad manners or sloppy work. I always expected the people I worked with to be considerate to me, to their co-workers and, of course, to our customers. I'm a nut on what I call calendar integrity. I want meetings to start on time, and I want everyone who's supposed to participate to be there. I want my phone calls returned, my memos answered and deliveries made when promised. People who can't do those things have no business in a sales-oriented, customer-driven company. Personally, I don't know what business they do belong in.

"A company can't give good service—not what I consider good service—unless its people are committed to calendar integrity. Everyone who ever worked for me knows exactly what that term means to me. They know that when they have an appointment with me and are late—even a few minutes late—I don't let it slide by. It's not the few minutes that matters; it's the lack of respect for somebody else's time. I come down hard on those who do not perform the simple courtesies and tasks, and I'm consistent.

"If you don't return phone calls promptly or answer your mail quickly, if you break appointments at the last minute, without a darned good reason, or have people sitting on their hands because you're late for appointments you do keep—what kind of message are you sending out?" Rogers asks. "You're saying, 'Hey, customer, you're not really very important to me or my company.' I'll tell you this—I wouldn't want to do business with you. If I'm not sure you'll return my phone calls, how can I feel sure you'll expedite my order?

"I wonder about the ability of people who don't have the time to answer letters and return phone calls. My job kept me as busy as anyone in our business, but I always found time to respond to customers' letters or phone calls within a day. If I was traveling, an assistant let them know when I'd respond—and I don't think I ever made a liar out of anyone. If I told a customer I'd phone him by a certain time, and found that for some reason I couldn't, that customer received a call from my office. If I discovered I'd be late for an appointment—

even a few minutes late—whoever expected me was notified. I respected my customers' time just as I respected my own."

Be on time for every appointment, no matter who it is with—a customer, distributor, manufacturer or anyone else. If you show up as much as five minutes late for an appointment with a customer, he or she has probably already convinced himself or herself that you are not coming. Being there on time is critical to the sales process because people are impatient. People hate to wait, and rightfully so. If you know you will be late for an appointment, exercise common courtesy.

Don't start off on the wrong foot with a customer. Life is easier if you do things right the first time around. A wise person once said, "When you hit a home run, you can take your time running the bases."

REMEMBER

160. Whenever possible, write a personalized thank-you note instead of writing it on a word processor.
161. You can never say thank-you enough to a customer.
162. Return every call quickly and promptly.
163. When a customer telephones, don't put him or her on hold for more than a few seconds. A customer on hold even for a minute could become irate, and may even hang up to seek business elsewhere.
164. Whether you operate a small or big company, the personal touch should always be a part of your modus operandi.

CHAPTER 28

Never Compromise on Quality

Customers expect a certain level of quality from every product or service they purchase. Many are even willing to pay more for it. When customers choose to buy from your company, they expect value and performance. If your product falls short of these expectations, your customers will be disappointed and may choose not to do business with you again. On the other hand, you will completely satisfy your customers if you meet or exceed their expectations. Meeting or exceeding customers' expectations defines your company's level of quality.

Your company represents a certain level of quality to your customer. This standard should be maintained and never compromised, regardless of how high or low on the quality scale your product or service falls. Every time you compromise this quality, you lower your standard.

Quality should be constantly improved to meet the customer's needs—needs that change over time. If your quality doesn't improve, you could lose your customers to your competition.

There is room for improvement in virtually every product. To see this, examine your product or service. Think about what purpose it serves and how long should it last. Of course, the proper level of quality needed will vary. For example, if your product is a coffee stir stick, it is used only once, then thrown away. It is not necessary to constantly work on improving this product, since it already serves its purpose well. If, on the other hand, your product is toothpaste, your competition is always developing new and improved products. You will have to constantly improve your product just to stay competitive.

Cheaper is not better

In every industry, your competition can offer a product for a lower price. They often do this by lowering the standard of quality. I set a certain level of quality for my company. My company succeeded by offering the most expensive product in the industry because our customers appreciated our quality and were willing to pay for the best. Our competition only offered lower prices and an inferior product.

For years, my employees and franchisees wanted me to consider offering a budget closet—a cheaper version of our regular model. They told me we could greatly expand our market by selling to people who couldn't afford our regular closets. I refused because I felt my customers wouldn't be satisfied with an inferior product even if it was less expensive. Also, anyone who bought a budget closet couldn't give a good referral—they would tell their friends our product was cheap but neglect to explain theirs was the budget model. A budget model would have cheapened our image. I was not willing to compromise my quality for more sales.

Employees and quality

Familiarize your employees with your company's standard of quality and stress it beginning the day they start. This level of quality is expected by your customer. Every time a substandard product ends up in the hands of a customer, your company standards are lowered.

Subway's quality

Subway, a chain of 8,000 restaurants offering submarine sandwiches, discovered it wasn't easy for stores in remote locations to find good, fresh bread, a basic ingredient they needed for sandwiches. This affected the entire system's quality.

"Remote stores were able to buy only bread made locally," Fred DeLuca, founder and CEO explains. "Frequently, this bread wasn't uniform or good-tasting. To ensure our product's quality, it became necessary to purchase a bread-making machine for each store, enabling them to make their own fresh bread every day. This was done because we knew our customers expected good sandwiches.

"The bread machines were very expensive," he continues. "It took a monumental amount of persuasion to convince our franchisees to invest in them."

DeLuca realized the difference in quality was reason enough to make the expense worthwhile.

"Our goal is to deliver the best quality product at the best price," he says, "but it is a delicate balancing act. As a result, we might not always deliver the highest quality of meat possible. Will we pay an extra dollar a pound for extra lean ham? Perhaps, but it depends on our customer's expectations. Sometimes, it is not cost-effective to pay the extra dollar. We strive to deliver to our consumers, the best value for the lowest price.

"Mercedes Benz might make the best quality automobile, but not everybody is willing to pay the price for it," points out DeLuca. "Not when they can buy a great car such as a Ford for a fraction of the cost!"

REMEMBER

165. Customers expect quality, value and performance.
166. Meeting or exceeding expectations will satisfy your customers.
167. Standards of quality should be maintained and never compromised. If you compromise your quality, you will lower your standards.
168. You have to constantly improve your product to stay competitive.
169. Employees should be familiar with your company's standards of quality.
170. Each time a substandard product ends up in the hands of a customer, your company standards are lowered.

CHAPTER 29

Quality Starts at the Top

Quality is the result of a personal commitment, balanced with desire and dedication, and is achieved when a customer's expectations are met or exceeded. To achieve a high standard of quality, a company must have a set of principles and practices enforced by its management and leader. As the owner, your intentions, though they may be good, are not enough. If you want to exceed your customer's expectations, you must be completely committed to performing and behaving in the manner required by your principles. You must set the standards for your company and uphold them with the same regard that you expect of your employees. Quality starts at the top and has to be felt right through to the bottom.

When a fish dies, it stinks from the head down. A company experiences the same phenomenon. When the leadership of a company doesn't observe its own high standards and principles, a bad business practice will permeate the company all the way down to the bottom ranks. On the other hand, when an organization is run very well, this is because it has strong leadership. An organization must be run by a leader who sets and observes the same high standards expected of subordinates. A leader cannot just preach quality, he or she must display it. As the company owner, you cannot tell your employees, "Do as I say, not as I do."

A strong company leader must effectively articulate the company's standards and principles to his or her employees. Every employee needs to know the level of quality expected. Once you set your standards, constantly remind your employees what they are. What use are high principles and standards of quality if your employees are not aware of them?

Quality throughout the company

It is very difficult to segment quality and observe it in selected parts of your business. If you want to operate a quality organization, the same high standards must be observed by every department within your company. This standard of quality is revealed through your products, the appearance of your stores, and how you treat your employees, suppliers and customers.

Don't ever compromise your standards in front of your employees because they will ultimately do the same to your customers. If your standards are lowered even one time, expect your employees to follow this example. If you ship a below-standard product to a customer, you send a message to your employees that this is acceptable and quality is not important to your company. Later, your employees will do the same to more customers. It is easier to lower your standards than it is to improve them. When you go down the quality scale, you develop new standards which, unfortunately, your employees will follow.

Quality management

Consider your level of quality every time you make a decision and make it apparent with everything you do, from the type of raw materials and equipment you purchase to your delivery methods. You must provide your people with the best tools and work environment possible so they can produce excellent quality work. Additionally, the way you treat your employees affects your success in business. If you treat them poorly, don't expect them to treat your customers any better.

Everybody can't be the best

Not every organization is able to offer top quality. For example, if your company is a discount chain, you will sacrifice high quality. Your customers won't expect it because your prices are low. It is difficult for a company to offer to its customers quality, service and price. You can't offer all three—it just doesn't work. If you want to offer your customers great quality and service, then you will have to charge a higher price for your product.

California Closet's high standards

What separated my company from my competitors was the high level of quality and service we offered our customers. We were the most expensive company and if the market was concerned only with the lowest price, we would have been out of business a long time ago. People were willing to pay fifteen to twenty percent more for a California Closet because we gave great service, the finest materials and lifetime warranties.

A quality product is a source of pride

Honda Motor Company's management practices what it preaches about the importance of quality. "What separates Honda and our people from many other organizations is that when it comes to quality, we never compromise. Never," a Honda executive once stated. "There is only one standard and it never varies.

"We always remember that no product, under any circumstances, ever goes out the door if quality is compromised," he explained. "We can't say, 'Okay, shipping must go on today. Just this one time we'll slacken our standards and let the car go out the door, and we'll hope and we'll pray it will go unnoticed.' If we do that, we've taught our people that a double standard exists, one that's dependent upon how management feels at a particular time.

"Once that has been done, you have violated your rules and lost sight of your real objective," he continued. "When this is lost, it is impossible to get back. Your people will be confused and will no longer understand what you truly want to accomplish."

Honda believes quality is a top priority, something that has precedence even over productivity.

REMEMBER

171. To achieve a high standard of quality, a company must have a set of principles and practices enforced by its management and leader.
172. If you want to operate a quality organization, the same high standards must be observed by every department within your company.
173. Don't ever compromise your standards in front of employees or they may do the same to your customers.
174. Consider your level of quality every time you make a decision and make it apparent with everything you do.

CHAPTER 30

Being a Team Player

Pity the business whose owner insists on running the company alone. Don't be an owner who wants to make all the decisions and ignores employee suggestions, and demands rather than asks.

A business owner must create a team. Your employees can commit to making your company successful only when they are involved in how the business is run. For employees, a paycheck isn't enough. They want jobs that give them responsibility, meaning and purpose. Employees who feel they are part of the whole perform better. By involving, listening to and appreciating your employees, you'll see results.

Team building

Everybody must work together as a team and share the same set of objectives. They must have a very strong sense of their individual involvement and contribution. A professional baseball team is a good analogy: Nine employees take the field, each covering his or her own territory, each with a special expertise—independent performers dependent on the rest for the best results. It is great when employees who work together do so in harmony. If they don't get along, if they pull in different directions or have communication problems, the

159

quality of their work suffers. Make no mistake, how well employees work together has a major impact on the company's success.

A great company requires great people. Even if you have the greatest product in the world, if you don't have terrific people selling and servicing the product, your business won't fly.

Your employees don't come to you as a team. It's up to you to mold them into one. Clearly communicate your corporate mission to your employees. They need to know that their common purpose is finding, keeping and satisfying customers. Then, explain to each employee his or her role in meeting this objective.

Once every employee understands how he or she contributes toward your objective, be supportive. Don't make an employee feel foolish for what he or she says, even if you don't agree with it. There's nothing wrong with disagreeing if you give an employee a chance to voice an opinion. Spend some time with employees and involve them, making them feel part of your decision-making process. Employees don't enjoy being told about changes, but if they are involved in decision-making, they respond favorably.

As the owner of the business, set a good example for your team by treating people fairly and honestly. Employees who see their boss cheating a customer or cutting corners will lose respect and may even follow the example.

Supporting the team

Every member must be supportive of the entire team. Employees who aren't supportive can hurt your business. I explained to my nonsupportive employees, "If you can't be supportive of one another...one of you will have to leave the company—maybe both of you." When I had employees who didn't want to be involved with the team, I had to get rid of them. I needed an environment where my employees—the team—could develop winning characteristics. I put my foot down and kept it down. I didn't let one or two "bad apples" spoil the whole bunch.

Sharing rewards

If your company enjoys success, share the rewards with your team. The surest way to discourage employees is by giving credit to only a few. Don't let a handful of employees hog the applause—they didn't win alone! Be generous with praise for every team member who helped your company be successful.

Reward employees for good performance with constant feedback and positive reinforcement—this is crucial when building a winning team. Your reinforcement will make employees care about their performance. Recognize employees who improve their performance and reward progress in a meaningful way. The praise you bestow on employees goes a long way toward building their confidence.

An important part of team-building is using the team to plan your company's future. I brought all my employees together and involved them in my decisions. I spent a lot of time talking to them, from the carpenters to the salespeople—and asking how they would solve our problems. Nobody knows the job better than the person who does it! A team of 10 enthusiastic employees accomplishes more than 100 unenthused individuals. This is why bringing employees together as a team is so important—working together makes it all happen.

REMEMBER

175. Employees perform better if they feel part of the whole. By involving, listening to and appreciating employees, you'll see results.
176. Everybody must work together as a team, sharing the same set of objectives.
177. To build a great team, hire the right people.
178. Clearly communicate your corporate mission to employees. They need to know their common purpose—finding, keeping and satisfying customers. Explain each employee's role in meeting this objective and how they can accomplish this.
179. Spend some time with employees asking for their opinions. Involve employees, and make them feel part of the decision-making process.
180. Set a good example for your team. Treat people fairly and honestly. If employees see you cheating a customer or cutting corners, they'll lose respect and may even follow your example.
181. Share rewards with your team. Reward each employee for good performance with constant feedback and positive reinforcement.
182. A team of 10 enthusiastic employees accomplishes more than 100 unenthused individuals.

CHAPTER 31

Hiring the Right People

The people you employ have the power to make or break your business. This makes your hiring decisions extremely important. While you may wish to hire the best people, unfortunately, you can't. You can hire only the best available people. Unless you hire a headhunter to locate a seasoned veteran, you will be limited to hiring only the people who apply for the opening.

Start your employee search far in advance of your need. Don't wait until you are so desperate to fill the position that you are forced to hire the first candidate you interview. It is a good idea to be constantly on the lookout for potential candidates, even when you have no openings. Invest in your company's future by continuing to interview interesting candidates. Keep their resumes on file just in case.

It is better for your employees to help your business grow than for your business to train your employees. In other words, hire a level above what you really need. Instead of hiring someone who knows how to run a $1 million business, hire someone with experience operating a $30 million business, because they have seen growth before and know how to handle it. This helps you avoid one of the most difficult decisions you will have to make during your career—replacing a long-time employee the company has outgrown, or hiring a new manager to oversee an old one. The veteran may have done a very good job, may even be a good friend, but he or she doesn't possess the necessary expertise to help operate a large company.

How to recruit

Finding really great employees is a difficult thing for me. With few exceptions, the best people are usually already employed. After all, a good, enthusiastic, hardworking person should never be out of work. The jobs are out there for good people, and there's usually a reason someone is unemployed.

A person's potential for success in your organization can be predicted by their skills and their level of motivation. To evaluate their skills, verify your candidate's work history, training and education. A person's motivation level is harder to pinpoint, but may be observed during the interview process. The best employees are the ones who enjoy what they do. Your task is to find people who really want to do the job and will take pleasure in it.

Using headhunters

Headhunters are often used to find an employee with a specific background. While I have found a few great employees through headhunters, I've also hired some who didn't work out. One disadvantage to headhunters is the high cost. To fill an upper-level management position paying $75,000 to $100,000 a year, you may pay a headhunter anywhere from 15 to 30 percent of the first year's salary plus benefits. I was fortunate enough to find most of my best people through word-of-mouth. I found them through friends, associates, or by recruiting them away from competitors and suppliers. You should hire the very best people possible, *however* possible.

Diedre Moire, an executive recruiting firm specializing in biotech, insurance, pharmaceutical, engineering and manufacturing, searches for positions ranging from neurosurgeons to engineers for aerospace companies. "We typically charge between 25 to 35 percent of the first year's total compensation package," explains president Steve Reuning. "We calculate a fee taking into account the type of data bases we have to rent or tap into. We also consider the number of hours a consultant will have to spend searching for the ideal candidate."

Although an executive recruiter may be very expensive, some-times it is worth the price—it's better to spend the money and hire an ideal candidate, than hire the wrong person for the job!

How to interview

For upper-level management positions, I interview a qualified candidate two or three times before making a final decision. It works well to meet with them away from the office environment. You can take candidates to lunch, for a walk or to play golf. Try to break the ice and get them to relax. This is a good way to avoid the prepro-grammed answers you normally hear during an interview.

Before I hire a candidate, I inform him or her what to expect from the job and I point out all the negatives and the positives. I tell man-agement-level employees that they should not expect a 40-hour work week. I ask my candidates if they have any questions for me—this is a good way to learn their priorities.

References are a poor way to evaluate potential employees, because candidates don't list employers who have anything negative to say. Additionally, employers who fear litigation will not criticize a former employee.

Steve Reuning believes most companies go about the interview process in the wrong manner. "The most common mistakes made when interviewing include having the wrong person conducting the first interview, not using a formal questionnaire and interviewing from the candidate's resume.

"First, the company chooses the wrong employee to conduct the initial interview," he explains. "The executives are aware that many candidates will apply for the job. They want the pool to be weeded out before they spend any time interviewing. So they choose a person whose time can be spared for the task. Typically, the person they choose is an administrative assistant, incompetent to conduct such an interview.

"So, the first screening an $80,000 to a $110,000 salaried person experiences is with an individual who's generally not trained to con-duct an interview," Reuning exclaims. "A really great applicant with the best talents—the person who you really want to hire—is going to be insulted that this is the person the company chose to conduct the interview. Even worse, the administrative assistant assigned to the task will probably not be able to recognize the difference between an ideal candidate and a poor or mediocre candidate.

"As a result, many companies try unsuccessfully to recruit on their own, and later hire my company to do the project for them," the recruiter says. "Often, the first two or three ideal candidates my company finds for the position tell us, 'I already applied for this job, but was turned down immediately!' When I have brought this to a company's attention, I always find out an administrative assistant rejected the applicant because the resume didn't list six of the eight requirements on the checklist for the position. Well, a resume doesn't tell the whole story—you have to interview to learn about a candidate!

"I have learned from experience, to *never* interview from a candidate's resume," continues Reuning. "People who don't know how to interview ask questions based on the resume. This is a mistake because they hire a person based on their ability to write a good resume. The best way to interview is by using a list of standardized questions that are derived from the job description, so you can compare apples to apples and not apples to oranges.

Once you have found the right person

Pay top dollar for your top people. What a valuable investment! If you have a choice between hiring two mediocre employees at $40,000 each or one good, experienced person at $80,000, choose the latter— offering them bonuses and incentives besides. It is important to make a valuable employee happy by paying him or her well and providing job security.

Provide your new employee with an orientation the very first day on the job. The orientation should be thorough, and introduce your corporate philosophy, objectives, values and principles. Discuss your employee's career path, regardless of his or her position on your corporate ladder. This is just as important for you. Additionally, on a semiannual or annual basis, each employee should be reviewed by his or her immediate supervisor and a group of his or her peers.

REMEMBER

183. Start searching for employees in advance. Be on the lookout for potential candidates, even when you have no openings.
184. It is better for your employees to help your business grow than for your business to train your employees. In other words, hire employees at a level above what you really need.
185. A person's potential for success as a part of your organization is indicated by his or her skills and level of motivation.
186. Find people who really want to do the job and will take pleasure in it.
187. Pay as much as you can afford to for your top people. This is always a valuable investment.
188. The most common mistakes made when interviewing include having the wrong person conducting the first interview, not using a formal questionnaire and interviewing from the candidate's resume.
189. The best way to interview is by using a list of standardized questions that are derived from the job description, so you can compare apples to apples and not apples to oranges.
190. Hiring is a terrific gamble. Unfortunately, you never know exactly the type of employee this person is going to be until after you have already hired him or her.

CHAPTER 32

The Art of Communicating

Though communicating seems easy enough, it is not. You must be able to effectively communicate with your employees your vision, goals and company priorities. To be an effective communicator, you must first think through what you want to say so you avoid sending a confusing message.

Good communication is concise, simple and factual. Is there anything worse than having to listen to a long, drawn-out speech? A good communicator makes a message understood in as few words as possible. Tell them what you are going to tell them, tell them, then tell them what you told them.

Whether you talk or write to your employees, say your most important points first or last. Do not bury what you are trying to say in the middle of a long-winded speech. Your employees pay the greatest attention at the beginning and end of what you say.

After you deliver a message to your employees, listen to their feedback. If they don't respond, chances are they probably didn't understand what you said.

The art of listening

Communication is a two-way street. As your employees must listen to what you say, you must listen to them. A good manager is a good listener. If you don't listen to your people, you lose their confidence. Not only listen, but acknowledge what they have said and then respond. If you don't use their advice, explain why you didn't. If you ignore your employees or don't acknowledge what they say, they will stop coming to you.

When your employees talk, you may need intuition to understand what they mean. Because they may feel uncomfortable telling you negatives, they will do so in a roundabout way. Can you read between the lines?

If you invite your employees to discuss problems with you, they can often help you find solutions. Managers who try to solve problems by themselves waste a valuable resource. Employees who face the issue at hand on a daily basis should be consulted before solutions are implemented.

It's especially important to keep open lines of communication with employees who have direct contact with your customers, such as those in sales and marketing. To be responsive to your customer's needs, listen to the employees who maintain closest contact with the market.

Effective communication involves every single employee of a company. I found that a good way to communicate back and forth with my employees was through informal discussions in small groups. The more informal the meeting, the more comfortable my employees felt telling me how *they* felt. Not only were they happy to have the opportunity to meet and talk with me, what I learned from these meetings was often invaluable.

REMEMBER

191. Talk about your vision, goals and company priorities with your employees.
192. A good communicator makes a message understood in as few words as possible. Tell them what you are going to tell them, tell them, then tell them what you told them.
193. Communication is a two-way street. A good manager is a good listener.
194. Invite your people to discuss problems with you so they can help you find solutions.

CHAPTER 33

The Art of Decision-Making

It's best to face the music at decision time. As the owner of a business, the worst thing you can do is procrastinate when you need to make a decision. You must be capable of making decisions quickly, but not hastily, allowing yourself the time needed to carefully analyze the whole picture.

Involve your people

Since you will make decisions every day, what is the best way to make a decision? First, look objectively at the decision to be made, then solicit opinions from your employees. Large companies encounter problems when their executives push hasty decisions through, without input from the employees, suppliers, manufacturers or customers who are directly affected.

Through experience, I realized it's important to solicit opinions from those involved with the issue at hand. Those involved in the decision-making process are more likely to support the final decision, even if they don't initially agree. If your employees are forced to accept a decision without being given a chance to make suggestions, the change will never work the way you hoped. Before I make a decision, I evaluate the suggestions made by my employees and create a balance sheet—looking at every advantage and disadvantage.

Bad decisions

In the past, I made bad decisions when I was upset or I didn't take time to think things over carefully. Hasty decisions come when you don't step back and go through your normal decision-making process that usually serves you so well. Every decision affects your future. Think about where each decision will lead. Establish a decision-making process for yourself and stick to it. For example, take a step backwards and review your options. This will help keep you from making bad decisions.

Avoiding decision

One day, you will be faced with making a tough decision. Don't be afraid and procrastinate—this is the worst thing you can do. A bad decision is better than no decision at all—you have to do something.

Whenever you have a decision to make, create a deadline for yourself. Rarely will your people agree unanimously, but they will be forced to compromise if there is a deadline. Once the decision is made, let your employees know you expect them to support it.

Consider your alternatives

Just as you don't make a decision when you are upset or angry, don't allow yourself to be forced by anyone to make a decision hastily. Give yourself a little time and ask for alternatives. If you are told there aren't any, tell the person to come back when they have one to give you. Do not move forward until you are given one. Since I believe there is an alternative for every decision, I always challenge people to think of different ways to do things. Often, a person asking for a quick decision has a hidden agenda, so take time to think things through. The expression "Ready, fire, aim!" doesn't work. It's "Ready, aim, fire!" Take the time to aim before you fire.

Quick decision-making

What an advantage to be nimble and quick and able to turn on a dime! Lightness of foot—the ability to change and adapt and make quick decisions—is a great asset for an entrepreneur. So, when you have little time to make a critical decision, you must have people you rely on to provide recommendations. In a pinch, stop everything else you are doing and focus on nothing else. Pull your assets together and review your alternatives so you can make the best choice possible.

Hindsight is better than foresight. Don't expect to make the right decision every time. I sure didn't, but that is part of owning a business. As your company grows, too, you may notice decision-making becoming more complicated. But if you take time to solicit opinions of people affected by the decision, and carefully analyze all the alternatives, the decision you make will be the best possible at that time.

REMEMBER

195. Don't procrastinate when you must make a decision.
196. Before you make a decision, solicit the opinions of those facing the issue at hand.
197. Employees will be more likely to support decisions if they are involved in the decision-making process.
198. Establish a decision-making process for yourself and stick to it.
199. Whenever you have a decision to make, create a deadline for yourself.
200. A bad decision is better than no decision at all.
201. Don't allow yourself to be forced by anyone to make a decision hastily. Give yourself a little time and ask for alternatives.
202. Lightness of foot—the ability to change and adapt and make quick decisions—is a great asset for an entrepreneur. Pull your assets together and review your alternatives so you can make the best choice possible.
203. Don't expect to make the right decision every time.

CHAPTER 34

The Effective Boss

An effective leader is one who knows what needs to be done to accomplish goals. This leader is focused, manages his or her time by delegating to employees, and is a motivator, spreading enthusiasm throughout his or her business.

The most successful leaders recognize their strengths and weaknesses and allow employees to help make decisions. They say no when necessary, yet they don't hide behind a policy. Last but not least, they don't take themselves too seriously.

The most important words to remember
There are several important words I have revered throughout my career as an entrepreneur and an effective leader:

The six most important words: I admit I made a mistake.
The five most important words: You did a great job!
The four most important words: What is your opinion?
The three most important words: If you please.
The two most important words: Thank you.
The one most important word: We.
and finally, the least important word: I.

The boss isn't always right...

When it comes to running a business, no one makes the right decisions all the time—not even the boss! We are all human and humans make mistakes. As a boss, you will make the best decisions possible if you understand your personal strengths and weaknesses and allow others to help you.

...but he's still the boss

A boss isn't always right, but he or she is still the boss and has to make many decisions. It is unrealistic for employees to think their boss is going to make the right decisions all the time, but at the same time, they should support each decision, regardless of their personal beliefs.

It is essential that you share a mutual respect with your employees. Don't be a tyrant who demands, "I am the boss and this is the way we are going to do it." Instead, say "I appreciate your support to do things my way—let's do it together."

Saying no

From time to time, you will have to say no to an employee's request—you can't say yes all the time. Saying no is a part of being a manager, something you'll learn to do if you haven't already.

Saying no is very difficult, something many leaders avoid. It's no fun rejecting an employee's idea or request, but it's something you must do from time to time. Saying no is an unpleasant task, but it can be done in a gentle way. For example, an employee asks to take a couple of days off at a bad time. You reject the request, explaining the reason why. If the employee understands the reasons behind your decision, he or she will understand why and accept the negative answer.

When an employee requests something you know immediately you will reject, don't procrastinate the decision. Never tell an employee, "I want to think about it," if you know what the answer is—this is the worst thing you can do. When an answer is no, it's much easier to say it right away. When an employee hears "Let me think about it," he or she has false hopes and anticipates hearing the answer he or she wants. I have learned from experience that false hope builds a larger disappointment later. When an employee hears a rejection immediately, he or she may be upset, but will move on. Learn how to say it, and say it quickly. Put it behind you rather than letting it eat at your gut all day. If you procrastinate, you'll make it more difficult for yourself later.

Never hide behind a policy

When a boss tells an employee, "Well, I would let you do it, but I can't because of company policy," he or she is avoiding making a decision. Leaders should make decisions and accept the fact that some will anger employees. Hiding behind a policy is nothing more than a cop-out. If a policy is fair, the manager should say, "I honestly think following this guideline is the right thing to do."

Company policies are guidelines, but typically have negative connotations and are not employee-friendly. Policies should be discretionary—not laws to live by. When employees complain that a policy is unfair, it should be reconsidered. This is more difficult to do in a large business. Most corporate giants operate in a formal style, subscribing to dozens of policies because of the number of employees. On the other hand, a small to medium-sized company is able to be more flexible and loose—modifying, adding and deleting policies quickly.

Policies can stagnate employees, restricting them from taking risks. Don't let this happen to your company. Employees who walk around scared of going against a policy, are worried about the wrong thing—they should be concerned with what they can do to help achieve company goals.

Don't take yourself too seriously

The most positive office environment is one that is high-energy with enthusiastic employees who want to achieve company goals. It is difficult to achieve this type of environment with a boss who takes himself or herself too seriously. Believe it or not, plenty of business owners act so serious you'd think they were the President of the United States!

Every business has its own personality, created by its leader. Of course, some businesses lend themselves to serious management, for example, law and accounting firms. But, as the leader of your company, you have the power to develop the personality you want for your office environment. If you walk around your office with a long face, you set a mood for your people. The more enjoyable and positive you can make your working environment for employees, the more motivated, productive and enthusiastic they will be. Employees who enjoy their working environment develop team spirit, while you enjoy a lower turnover rate.

REMEMBER

204. As a boss, you will make the best decisions possible if you understand your personal strengths and weaknesses, and those of your employees.
205. A boss isn't always right, but he or she is still the boss, required to make many decisions. Once a decision is made, employees should support it.
206. It's essential that you share mutual respect with your employees.
207. From time to time, you will have to say no to an employee's request.
208. When an employee requests something you know you will reject, don't procrastinate. When the answer is no, say it right away.
209. Company policies should be discretionary—not laws to live by.
210. Policies can stagnate employees, restricting them from taking risks.

CHAPTER 35

Leading By Example

As the owner of the company, you set the standards for your employees. You're the coach of this team, with a responsibility to provide guidance for each subordinate. You're responsible for establishing your company's ethical standards as well as quality, service and energy levels. When you lead by example, you'll gain—respect from your employees.

Do as I say, do as I do

Effective managers practice what they preach! Employees follow in the owner's footsteps, and recreate behaviors they witness. An owner who declares a company policy to drastically reduce unnecessary expenses and then charters an airplane at the company's expense for an extravagant trip to the Caribbean won't inspire cost-cutting among support staff. To enforce a policy, the owner must abide by the same rules as the employees. Employees who witness company leaders following company goals and policies, tend to respect them and do the same.

Setting the tone

The leader sets the tone for the entire company. Employees emulate their leaders, from the way they dress to the hours they work. A vivacious owner will have energetic employees. On the other hand, a boss who's serious and formal will have employees who act that way, too. Be excited, enthusiastic, positive and confident about your goals. If you are committed to excellence and continuous improvement, your employees will be, too.

Employees watch every move you make. If they see you leave work everyday at 4:00 p.m., they'll lose the desire to work their hardest. Employees prefer a boss who works as hard, if not harder, than they work. They prefer a boss to be accessible, observing and supporting their efforts, rather than a boss who comes in late, takes long, leisurely lunches, and is on vacation constantly.

When you have a bad day, don't let your mood affect how you treat people. If they see you upset, you may appear weak to them. To keep their confidence, you need to keep your chin up, be strong and create a positive working environment.

It is your responsibility to charge your company's atmosphere with excitement and optimism. Your attitude, positive or negative, rubs off on your employees. Unfortunately, many people in leadership positions are terrible role models. They enervate rather than energize people. A winning attitude around your employees will go through to the customers they serve.

The Smiley style

My nickname is Smiley because I always smile. I find it easier to smile than to frown. My mood sets the tone for my work place and it's contagious! How much easier it is to be friendly and warm than distant and cold! When you are friendly to employees, they like and respect you more and work harder for you. You'll enjoy lower turnover. If you treat employees poorly, they will treat customers the same way or even quit altogether. Employees react more positively to an enthusiastic leader who smiles than to another who frowns all day long.

REMEMBER

211. You're responsible for establishing your company's ethical standards as well as quality, service and energy levels.
212. Effective managers practice what they preach!
213. To enforce a policy, the owner must abide by the same rules as the employees.
214. The leader sets the tone for the entire company. Employees emulate their leaders, from the way they dress to the hours they work.
215. Be excited, enthusiastic, positive, and confident about your goals.
216. When you have a bad day, don't let your mood affect how you treat your people.
217. Employees react positively to an enthusiastic leader. Enthusiasm is contagious!

CHAPTER 36

How to Manage, But Not Control, Your Employees

Some entrepreneurs want to control every aspect of their company. They demand to write the music, play the instruments, lead the band, and be the producer all at the same time! This will destroy the company! As the leader, you shouldn't be a part of every decision nor should you have complete control over the actions of your employees. Yes, control your company, but don't micro-manage every single process. Your employees must be allowed to grow and flourish. You merely inspire and lead them to achieve and accomplish the company's goals.

Allow your employees room to develop. If you over-supervise, you stunt their growth. Even worse, if you are a self-conscious manager, eyeing their every move with suspicion and insecurity, they will be afraid of making a mistake. You want your employees to take chances, so allow them to make mistakes. If you have hired the right people, you'll trust and respect their abilities. Treat them with respect, and you build self-esteem. When you over-control them, you will not get the best out of them.

As the leader, you need to clearly communicate the company goals and how you expect each employee to contribute. When they make mistakes, inform them in a positive and constructive manner. The more self-confidence and self-esteem your employees have, the better they perform at their jobs.

Allowing employees to make mistakes

A boss who wants to make every decision is a bad boss. A good boss helps his or her employees make good decisions. I encourage my employees to make their own decisions. I might guide them in the right direction, but I don't tell them what to do. Sometimes I know they are making the wrong decision, because I have made many of the same mistakes myself, but I know this is the only way they will grow as employees. The worst thing you can tell an employee is, "I told you so." You don't need to remind an employee he or she made a mistake. Allow your people to do things their own way, while you help them get where you want them to be.

Management by intimidation can destroy a company's positive energy. Instead, manage your staff through motivation. Make people feel good about their jobs. They'll take that positive energy and use it to do their jobs better.

The great game of business

Jack Stack, CEO of Springfield Remanufacturing Corporation (SRC) and author of *The Great Game of Business*, developed a strategy to manage his employees—teaching them the total concept of how a business works.

"We (the management at SRC) made a promise to ourselves that we would teach everybody who works for us how business works," he explains. "Skills are important, but it's more important for people to understand the total concept of how a business works. We teach them how they make a difference with their day-to-day performances, by teaching them the rules of the game of business, and we give them a stake in the outcome.

"We tell employees, 'Look, we can spend the rest of our lives in the trenches trying to arm-wrestle a 4- to 5-percent wage increase every year, or we can try to develop the company and let the market pay the higher wages.

"In 1983, we began to teach the employees the game of business," he says. "In doing so, we developed a very high intellectual community. We found out that the more inspired our employees became, the more questions they asked and the more they began to drive the organization. The more we learned, the more there was to learn.

Through the application of economic literacy, disregarding the whole concept of 'You have to do your job, nothing more, nothing less,' your people can act and feel like owners," he continues. "When an employee's self-esteem grows, he or she will be more productive.

"We have many awareness programs and we meet with employees for an hour every week to go over all the financial details of the company," Stack says. "In the meetings, we ask our people what we are doing wrong and ask them to submit in writing areas where we need to improve. We tell them, 'If you think of a better way to do something...do it!' "

According to Stack, establishing reachable goals is an important part of managing employees. "We set goals and then teach our employees how to achieve them. We tell them how they can make a difference and an impact. And we always let our employees make mistakes—that's how they learn."

Helping employees grow

According to Doug Mellinger, president of PRT Corporation of America, a software re-engineering firm based in New York City, his management style has changed and developed since he started the business.

"In the early days, I used to drive everything that went on in the company and followed my employees' every step," he recalls. "Back then, I was the driver, not the navigator. After counseling with my mentors, studying management books, and taking several management courses, I learned I wasn't doing the right thing to grow to the next level.

"As the company grew, I also took the necessary steps to educate each employee on what was going on in the company," Mellinger continues. "I was shocked to find out most of my employees didn't even understand the difference between cash flow and receivables! They didn't know the basics of what was going on in the company. They knew only what their own area was—whether it was marketing or administrative. So, I developed a program in which an employee representing each department in the company would teach, on a biweekly basis, the other departments, all about their job and responsibilities."

Mellinger wanted to make his company more efficient. To do so, he created teams of employees who meet on a weekly basis to analyze the company. "The teams work on creating the future for the company," he says. "There are no rules and anything can be changed. This has radically changed the company because it has encouraged my people to take an initiative. They are coming up with ideas and solutions I would never think of."

According to the president, the teams have improved the company dramatically, helping it achieve many goals. "Our morale is higher," he exclaims, "and our profits and sales are better than ever! Because we hit so many goals, I gave every employee in the company an equal share of a portion of the profit as a bonus.

"My people realize they are the drivers who make the changes," he adds. "When my company has problems, everybody attacks them together. We have all but eliminated the individual, and are team-oriented now. I have allowed my employees to grow, and so will my company, with their help."

REMEMBER

218. As the leader, you shouldn't be part of every decision, nor should you have complete control over your employees' actions

219. Your employees must be allowed to grow and flourish—you merely inspire and lead them to achieve and accomplish the company's goals.

220. If you hired the right people, you will trust and respect their abilities.

221. The more self-confidence and self-esteem your employees have, the better they will perform.

222. Allow your people to do things their own way, within reasonable limits, while you help them get where you want them to be.

223. Management by intimidation destroys a company's positive energy.

224. Be upfront with conflict and always be fair in dealings with employees.

225. Make decisions that are fair, reasonable and in the best interest of the group.

226. Let your employees make mistakes—that's how they learn!

CHAPTER 37

Being a Risk-taker

There is an element of risk in every new business. A business owner eats risk for breakfast! Don't be afraid of failure. Risks are necessary for a growing business. Consider each risk a possible opportunity. You will never be successful if you never take a chance.

You have set many goals for your business. Each goal involves risk—some more than others. The only way to accomplish goals is to be fearless in the face of failure! Every successful entrepreneur has had some failure because of risks taken. Some risks work out for the best, while others are costly—but you never know until after you take it!

Everybody makes mistakes!

If you are determined to find success, you must be willing to make mistakes along the way. It may surprise you to learn that many successful companies took risks and experienced failures while trying to develop new products. Pepsi Cola, for example, went bankrupt three times before it became profitable.

When Life Savers introduced the ever-popular candy, it was the laughingstock of the entire candy industry! Who ever heard of a hard candy with a hole in the middle? Now the company successfully markets the "holes" as an additional product line! When Kleenex first developed its tissue paper, it was marketed as an upscale beauty aid. The early advertisements promoted its use as a disposable substitute for face towels. Kleenex failed to find its niche in this market, and sales lagged for many years until it was remarketed as a substitute for the pocket handkerchief. The ad campaign was adjusted to say, "Don't put a cold in your pocket." Only after the product was reintroduced did it find success.

Learning from mistakes

Learn from your mistakes—perhaps a small adjustment the next time around may bring the results you want. What you learn from a mistake can be valuable. Successful entrepreneurs learn from their mistakes and use the experience to their benefit. You can learn from every mistake—something that will strengthen you in the future. Just don't let the failure discourage you from trying again.

Confronting adversity

Adversity surrounds every entrepreneur with a growing business. You don't face it alone—it happens to everybody. What separates you from the failures is how you handle adversity. Successful entrepreneurs handle adversity head-on, while others avoid taking risks and back off.

Managing risk

Are the rewards worth risking failure? What effects might possible failure of a risk have on your company? You can manage the risks you take by understanding what they are and what is at stake. Only then, will you be able to determine if the risk is worth taking. Examine your goal and see if the risk is worth the possible results.

If you choose to take the risk, limit the downside by doing your homework. Prepare yourself and find ways to limit the risk. You may even choose to involve your people by developing the idea—the risk—with their support. Their opinions may help you set your boundaries for the risk at hand.

Allowing employees to take risks

Risk-takers are important not only at the top of the organization, but at every level throughout the entire company. Encourage your employees to be innovative and take managed risks—to come up with new ideas and ways to do their jobs. Don't instill fear of risk in your employees; this will discourage them from challenging themselves.

To promote the entrepreneurial spirit, International Business Machines allows its employees to take risks. The company gives its employees a great deal of authority and responsibility in their jobs. The corporate giant believes that its people need the freedom to experiment. Management understands that employees will make their share of mistakes, but they will also learn how to deal with them. If the employee is successful, it can benefit the company tremendously. IBM realizes that success is found only after certain risks are taken.

Risky business

McDonald's Corporation, with more than 13,000 restaurants in 65 countries, wouldn't be the success it is today without the entrepreneurial spirit that is encouraged within the licensee system. Many of the new innovations, pivotal for the company's evolution into the fast-food service organization, were those of its licensees—entrepreneurs who knew exactly what the consumers wanted. New products that were introduced by licensees became the most important and successful additions to the menu in the history of the company.

For example in 1964, licensee Lou Groen, who owned a McDonald's in a predominantly Catholic neighborhood in Cincinnati, Ohio, saw his restaurant filled with customers six days a week. But on Fridays, his store was empty. The licensee realized that on this particular day, observant Catholics eat fish, which killed the hamburger sales.

Groen surmised that a fish sandwich would attract more business on Fridays.

"I've got to have a fish product; otherwise, I can't afford to stay open on Friday's," he told the management. His request was flatly denied: "We are in the hamburger business, not the seafood business!" The only way the frustrated licensee felt he could convince the corporate office to see things his way was to prove to them that fish sandwiches could be a profitable business.

Groen developed a sandwich using existing McDonald's equipment made with a piece of breaded halibut served in a hamburger bun. He took his recipe to the corporate office and made a sample for the corporate executives. After tasting it, they were extremely impressed and granted Groen permission to test-market the product at his restaurant. The sandwich was an immediate success and volume at Groen's store rose 30 percent within a year.

After a year of experimentation, a modified version of the sandwich was developed and permanently added to the menu at every McDonald's in the country. The Filet-O-Fish sandwich, an innovation of a single franchisee, became a standard menu item, which 30 years later, continues to be popular at McDonald's around the world.

The Big Mac, now a McDonald's institution, was also the innovation of an enterprising franchisee who wanted to increase business. Jim Delligatti, an operator in Pittsburgh, owned a unit in a heavily industrialized area, near several large steel mills. Every day, the restaurateur listened to dozens of complaints from laborers who said their appetites weren't satisfied by a single hamburger or cheeseburger. Delligatti realized the menu needed a "monster" sandwich for these workers, so he developed the Big Mac: a double-decker sandwich containing two hamburger patties, lettuce, onions, pickles, cheese and a special mayonnaise-based sauce. In 1968, he took the sandwich to the corporate office and convinced management to taste it. The colossal sandwich was so well-received that, after some modifications at company headquarters, it gained a permanent place on the menu.

According to Burt Cohen, vice president of licensing, "Experimentation has been very healthy for the system, and we encourage it from our employees. Most of the major breakthroughs in our menu line were made by franchisees."

Business is a gamble

Bill LeVine, founder of the PIP quick-printing company, remarks, "If you are not willing to take a risk, you will not be successful in business. Business is a gamble from day one—as the owner of a business, you have to gamble," he believes. "If you are not willing to take chances, you should not own a business.

"When taking a risk, you should always look at what the potential future is and jump at a great opportunity," the entrepreneur continues. "I would never have been so successful if I didn't jump at the opportunities I encountered. For example, when I first saw the ITEK camera, I bought it, and played around with it for a year. I took the chance of spending the money necessary to promote the product and it paid off—this was the technology that allowed me to create the quick print industry!

"I also took more risks when I looked for ways to embellish my locations to attract more customers," the founder explains. "For example, I placed copy and fax machines in each store well before they were marketed to the masses.

"Risk-taking never ceases to exist," LeVine adds. "It's part of owning and running every business!"

Nothing ventured, nothing gained!

Bill Trimble, president and CEO of the W.A.T. Capital Corp., a merchant banking and venture capital firm in Vancouver, British Columbia, faces risks every time he invests in a company. His philosophy is simple: "Nothing ventured, nothing gained!"

"People always take risks in business and in life in general," he explains. "You have to take what is perceived as a risk. A risk is something out of the ordinary—something you don't know or even understand. In my business, I take calculated risks and I believe there is much to be gained from these risks—even if they don't work out. There is lesson to be learned that may be invaluable.

"Before I take a risk, I calculate the risk versus the rewards," Trimble continues. "I always try to minimize my risks and avoid the over-risky ones that I perceive as too great to take."

REMEMBER

227. Every successful entrepreneur has had failures because of risks taken. Risk-takers are important not only at the top of the organization, but on every level throughout the entire company.
228. Encourage your employees to take managed risks—to come up with new ideas and ways to do their jobs.
229. Manage the risks you take by understanding what they are and what is at stake. Only then, will you be able to determine if the risk is worth taking.
230. If you choose to take the risk, limit the downside by doing your homework.
231. Learn from your mistakes—perhaps a small adjustment may produce the results you want the next time around.
232. Nothing ventured, nothing gained!

CHAPTER 38

The Art of Delegation

When your business is small, you are involved in every aspect of the daily activities at the office and your staff is slim. But, as your company grows, it will be time to stop doing everything yourself. You will need to free up time to attend to more important matters. To accomplish this, delegate some responsibilities to your employees.

If you are involved in every minute detail of your business you hurt—not help—your company. Many businesses fail because the owner is unwilling to delegate responsibilities to employees and tries to do everything himself or herself. It is impossible to do everything—there's just not enough time. If you hire the right people to work for you, you'll feel comfortable turning many responsibilities over to them.

When and how to delegate

When you first realize you need to free yourself for other matters that require your attention, proceed gingerly. The employee you choose to handle the delegated responsibility should be both capable and motivated.

Before you delegate, discuss with your employee exactly what you expect. So there will be no surprises, set guidelines and discuss expectations. Your employee should be aware of the quality and quantity of work that is expected and the deadline for its completion. Provide your employee not only with the materials they need but also the authority to do the job well. If you don't, you set him or her up for failure. Last but not least, step out of the way and let your employee get the job done!

Ask, do not tell, your employee to perform the task. You want your employee to be enthusiastic about taking on a new responsibility, and if he or she seems reluctant to accept it or will feel burdened by the task, don't request it. An employee forced into doing something rarely brings about a favorable outcome. The employee who wants and enjoys the new responsibility will produce better results.

Delegating to employees raises their self-esteem and makes them feel like a valued member of your team. New responsibilities help challenge and develop employees.

Avoid delegating a responsibility at the last minute. Give your employee as much notice as possible and expect him or her to take a little longer to complete the work than it might take you. Realize that the responsibility may be a new challenge to the employee. On a complicated issue, you may choose to delegate only a portion of it so the employee can learn the new task in stages. You don't want to give employees the impression you are dumping your work on them. They appreciate added responsibility more when you treat them as competent partners in your enterprise.

Delegating outside the business

Once you employ more than a few employees, you can consider jobbing out certain functions of your company—for example, payroll responsibilities. This tedious task typically requires three or more hours a week to complete. It may be cost-effective to hire a payroll service to do this for you. With a service, you call in each employee's gross monthly or weekly income. The service calculates all withholdings for you and processes your paychecks. Then you simply distribute the checks to your employees. This service can cost as little as $100 a month.

REMEMBER

233. If you are involved in every minute detail of your business you will hurt—not help—your company.
234. The employee you choose to handle a responsibility should be motivated as well as capable of the task.
235. Delegating responsibilities to employees raises their self-esteem.
236. New responsibilities challenge and develop employees. It may decrease turnover because your staff will be more satisfied with their jobs.
237. Discuss with your employee exactly what you expect. He or she should be aware of the quality of work expected, and the deadline for completion.
238. Ask, do not tell, your employee to perform the task. You don't want to give employees the impression you are dumping your work on them.

CHAPTER 39

How to Negotiate

Imagine yourself sitting at a table facing a potential supplier. You want to work out a deal, but do you know how to get what you want? Before you sit down to negotiate, regardless of the type of business transaction that will take place, there are many questions you should first ask yourself. Do you want to develop a long-term or a short-term relationship with the supplier? If it is a long-term relationship, then it is vital that you and your supplier both feel good about the negotiation and agreement. Some negotiators may pursue a deal that takes care of only their best interests. This works only if you never plan to do business with that supplier again!

Win-win negotiations

If you want to develop a long-term relationship with a supplier, it is critical to negotiate a contract that will be mutually beneficial. If you walk away from negotiations having everything in your favor, why would anyone want to do business with you in the future? The best way to negotiate is to leave something on the table.

When I negotiate with a new supplier, I never squeeze so hard that they don't get anything out of doing business with me. I want them to value me as a customer and I expect good service. If you negotiate a deal that doesn't allow the other party to make any money, you will be more of an annoyance than a good customer. The supplier has to make some money, too—that is why he or she is in business. Don't negotiate a deal that is one sided if you plan to do business with this firm again.

Throw-away verses important issues

Before you go into a negotiation, develop a plan of your priorities. You should have one list of issues that you want your own way, but you need a second list of throw-away issues—ones you're willing to concede.

When I negotiate, I am very passionate in the beginning about every issue, including the ones that are not significant to me. I make a big deal out of these throw-away issues because I know that when I do give in on them, the other party will feel they have won something. Then, I fight for what is really important to me. There are always some issues I will let go, and, in return, I get my way with the more important issues.

Before you negotiate, ask yourself, "What do I want to gain from this relationship." Do you want service, quality or price? Of course, you would like to have all three, but this is usually impossible. To me, quality and service are the most important issues. If I receive the quality product I want from a manufacturer or supplier, and excellent customer service, I will be more flexible about how much I will pay. During negotiations, most people talk about price first, but I don't until I am confident that quality and service issues are to my liking. If your only concern is getting the cheapest price, then quality and service cannot be important issues for your company.

Listen carefully

In negotiating, if you listen, they will talk. To find out exactly what the other party wants and what they are willing to give, allow them to do most of the talking. When people talk, they will always reveal more information than they planned to.

Honesty and sincerity

Be honest and sincere. You don't want to give the impression that what you say is deceptive. If you are perceived as sincere, the relationship will be healthier and more beneficial for you. If you are not trusted, you will be opposed on every issue.

Relationships are based on trust—no matter what the contract says. You spend hours negotiating a contract, and what becomes of it? It is filed away in a cabinet and retrieved only if there is a problem. Usually, contracts do not reflect the reality of a relationship. You will develop a routine with your supplier or customer, and you may stop following the contract by the letter. A contract is often nothing more than a guideline.

To build a good relationship with someone, you must prove you can keep your word and live up to your end of an agreement. A supplier or a customer who comes to realize there won't be any unpleasant surprises from you, wants to continue doing business with you, and may be even more flexible in the future. You want to build trust—this is vital for every good relationship.

Don't beat around the bush—be direct!

When you negotiate, it's easy to waste hours beating around the bush before approaching the real issues. Cut to the chase! Get important issues on the table quickly, before you exhaust yourself on minor ones. The primary issues first! While some people leave the most important issues for the end, I like to get them out in the open quickly so I know what I'm dealing with and how I'm going to make them work. Some people put just a few issues on the table at one time, negotiate them, then bring up a couple more and repeat the process. But if you know all the issues up front, you can choose some you'll be flexible with and others you won't compromise on.

Negotiating with a big ego

When negotiating with a person who has a big hungry ego, there is one way to successfully handle the situation: Feed it! The more you feed the ego, the more the person will like you, and the more the person likes you, the more he or she will give you in the negotiations!

I have often negotiated with people who had tremendous egos. Before we begin to negotiate the issues, I feed the ego by saying: "I have heard so much about you. I would love to do business with you." Of course it's true! I tell the person everything he or she hungers to hear. I want the person to think everything is his or her idea. I help the individual make the best decision, but at the same time, I guide the way to the decision I want. Then, I step aside and let the glory and accolades go to the other person.

There is no reason to fight a big ego. All you have to do is admire. There is a bottom line in negotiating. It is simple: People who like you, want to work with you and will give you the deal you want.

REMEMBER

239. To develop a long-term relationship with a supplier, it is critical to negotiate a contract that is mutually beneficial.
240. Leave something on the table every time you negotiate. If you walk away with everything in your favor, why would anyone do business with you again?
241. Before you enter a negotiation, list issues you want a specific way. You also need "throw-away" issues—ones you're willing to concede.
242. Before you negotiate, know what you want to gain from this relationship—service, quality or price.
243. If you are perceived as sincere, the relationship will be healthier and more beneficial for you. It is vital to build trust.
244. Long-term relationships secure a level of stability for your business.
245. When you negotiate, don't waste time avoiding the real issues. Discuss important issues first, then move on to secondary ones.
246. When negotiating with a big ego, there is one way to successfully handle the situation: Feed it!
247. The bottom line in negotiating is simple: If people like you, they will want to work with you and will give you the deal you want.

CHAPTER 40

The Value of Long-Term Relationships With Suppliers

Building a customer base while growing the business is a necessity for every business owner. This is impossible to achieve if you are wasting precious time replacing suppliers every month. Your suppliers can play a critical role in the success of your company, but only if they share a long-term relationship with you.

If you build a solid relationship with your suppliers, over the years, it can prove useful. If your company experiences a difficult period, you will be grateful to have long-term suppliers who stand by you. When you aren't able to pay bills and need extended credit, you will be able to call your supplier and say "Hey, I have a problem! How can you help me?" They may offer to delay your payment schedule or even reduce prices temporarily. Suppliers will help you in your times of need only if the relationship is long-term and based on trust.

I had outstanding relationships with my suppliers—many dated back to my earliest days in business. I was loyal to my suppliers because they had helped me out so many times over the years.

Show your appreciation by including suppliers in the success of your business. You can devise a compensation program based on performance. For example, you can offer stock options if your company is publicly owned.

Subway values its suppliers!

Fred DeLuca, founder and CEO of Subway, owes much of his company's early success to his suppliers. In 1966, the second year the company was in business, he had three stores—each unprofitable. The company was on the verge of going out of business.

Although profits were measly, DeLuca believed in his business and wanted to expand. Unfortunately, he had no credibility with the banks and couldn't borrow the capital he needed. "At the time, a low-priced store cost only around $1,000, while a high-cost store was $4,000 to assemble," the founder explains. "They were simple affairs—I could build each one with my own hands and furnish them with used equipment. Since the banks wouldn't loan me the money, I was forced to use the money I owed my suppliers! If it wasn't for them, Subway may not be what it is today.

"Back then, we had four suppliers in town—for bread, vegetables, meat and paper products. We paid them every Friday, but rarely enough to cover the whole bill.

"Each week, I drove around town, traveling from supplier to supplier to drop off a check in person," DeLuca continues. "I'd walk in and say to the owner, 'I have a $300 check for you. I realize it is not enough, but business was slow this week.' And then, I asked for more vegetables!

"Each supplier allowed me to do this because I was paying them on a regular basis and they liked seeing my face every week," DeLuca recalls. "My suppliers were very generous to extend this credit and did so because they trusted me. At the time, it was the only credibility we had!

"This credit enabled me to build the additional stores I needed," he exclaims, "and it was the new stores that pulled my company through the bad time. I am grateful for what they did for me."

REMEMBER

248. Suppliers can play a critical role in the success of your company if you have a long-term relationship.
249. Suppliers can help you in times of need.
250. Show suppliers your appreciation by including them in the success of your business.
251. Do not wait for your suppliers to call you when a payment is delinquent. When you have a problem, call them and avoid causing them anxiety.

CHAPTER 41

Growing Pains

As a business grows and expands, it experiences growing pains. As the owner and leader of the business, prepare for the transitions you'll face.

It is easier to manage a small business than a large business. Problems seem to get bigger as your company grows. When your business is small, everything runs smoothly and you have control over most decisions and daily activities. Once you expand, you run into problems. These are growing pains.

Financial planning for growth

Growth costs money and a growing business is like a monster—the more you feed it, the more it needs to eat. When your company begins to grow, to manage your cash flow closely, you'll need good financial planning. You will need to know in advance where your money will come from. Will it come from your cash flow or capital infusion? Never make financial commitments until you are sure you have the available capital. Many companies get into trouble by making commitments before they have actually raised the capital, only to discover they can't raise the money.

Hodgepodge growth

There are two types of growth—planned and unplanned. Hodge-podge growth is out-of-control, unmanaged and uncontrolled growth that can put a company out of business. My company experienced hodgepodge growth when we opened new stores randomly around the country. Our mistake was expanding without the use of a master plan.

In my first three years in business, my company grew from zero to $3 million a year. Our fourth-year sales were $7 million and by the eleventh year, we had grown to a $66 million business.

My first mistake during the early years of explosive growth, was to get into deals that didn't fit into my business plan. In addition, I kept on original employees who weren't experienced to handle the growth. To make matters worse, my financial management was uncontrolled—I had begun franchising the business, had dozens of stores around the world, but wasn't ready to service them. My company grew from a *medium* small business to a *large* small business—until it was a small *large* business.

My mentors and board of directors saved my company. They had experienced explosive growth and advised me, helping me make it through this difficult transition. Don't wait until your company is experiencing growing pains to put together a board of advisers or directors—do this when your company is still small. So when your company experiences unexpected growth, you'll have good advice and guidance to help you along, just as I did.

When the job outgrows an employee

As a business grows, it can quickly outgrow the people who run it. You may have a long-term employee who has been very devoted and hardworking, but is not experienced in handling additional responsibilities required when a business grows to a higher level. For example, when you started the business, you hired an accountant to be your assistant controller. As your business grows from $500,000 a year in gross sales to a $2 or $3 million a year level, this person might not be equipped with the necessary knowledge to handle a larger business. This is a difficult and emotional aspect of growing a business.

You will have many employees who started with you in the beginning—who stuck by you through all the difficult and trying times, and once the business outgrows their abilities—what do you do? It is your responsibility to hire a new person to take over the job. The original employee might deserve the opportunity, but you have to remind yourself it takes different types of people to do the same basic jobs at different levels of business. To avoid this, you should encourage your employees from day one to learn and grow by taking advanced business classes. You may even choose to hire a consultant to help train employees for greater responsibilities. If an employee is unable to or doesn't want to take on the new challenge, then it is your responsibility to hire a qualified person to take over the job. Of course it can be a very difficult decision, but you owe it to your employees, investors, customers, suppliers, manufacturers and yourself. This is why it is a good idea to hire above the level you really need so the employee can handle the job's responsibilities after the company has grown.

If you hire a manager from the outside, you might anger a long-time employee who feels deserving of the position. If growth is on your agenda, you can solve this problem ahead of time by designing an organizational chart that includes empty slots—above the positions for the people you have hired. If your employees know from the start that as the company grows, these higher level positions will eventually be filled with more experienced people, they will not be offended or surprised when it happens.

Keeping the enthusiasm

What I liked best when my company was small was the family atmosphere. People who work for smaller businesses are always more cooperative and enthusiastic. The trick is how to keep that same level of enthusiasm once the company has grown. Once your company grows from a small to medium-sized business, you enter a difficult transition—you will have to hire new employees and attempt to integrate them, make them part of the team.

Nothing will be the same

You will find that a business is easier to manage when it is small, and problems get bigger as the company grows. For example, when you hire people to manage new locations, the profits won't be the same as when you were running the show. No one will care as much as you about the business, so don't expect these stores to have the same productivity level as when you were there. Of course, this affects the success of the business.

For example, if you own a profitable dry cleaning store, and you decide to open a second unit, it probably won't be as profitable or productive as the first one. When you managed the store, you provided great service and you knew your customers because you were there all the time. The manager you hired for the new location won't run it as well as you or manage the expenses as tightly as you did—this is reality!

The problem will be magnified when you open more stores, because you'll have to spread yourself thinner and thinner, having less time to devote to each unit. The difference will be noticeable when you look over your balance sheets. If you made a 17-percent net profit at your original location, your second one will probably not be as profitable—13 percent, if you're lucky. Be realistic in your expectations!

Peaks and valleys

When the business was small, things were easy. But as the company expands, it will occasionally plateau. The difficulty is pulling out of this valley and reaching the next peak.

When my company grew and was selling $80,000 a month, it was less profitable than when it sold $60,000 a year earlier! This is because when the company was smaller, I had a small staff—a few installers and a couple of salespeople. To be able to sell $80,000 a month, I had to hire additional support. I discovered, with the additional employees, I couldn't make more profit until we hit $100,000!

Every company goes through these cycles. Sometimes a company will make more money with lower sales than it will when sales are higher. This happens to every business as it climbs to the next level. Even your personal income will drop during these valleys. Until you can get back up to that same profit level, you'll have to make some sacrifices. Growing a business doesn't come easy. If you want success, you have to be willing to pay for it.

Subway's peaks and valleys

Fred DeLuca, CEO of Subway, understands growth. In early 1987, his company had 991 stores. By the end of that same year, the company had doubled in size and had 1,810 units! According to DeLuca, this was a very difficult transition for his company.

"In just a few years, the company had grown from 200 stores to 300, 400 and 600," the entrepreneur says. "Then in 1987, we went from 991 to 1,810 units—all franchises. We grew 83 percent in less than 12 months!

"It was a difficult transition because opening so many franchises required a lot of support," he continues. "Not only did we have to recruit and train the new franchisees, but we also had to order new equipment and find additional locations! This was a challenging time because we didn't have enough trained staff in the office, and though we knew we would grow fast, we hadn't anticipated the demand. We had to make many changes very quickly to support this level of growth. And in doing so, we had to build a whole new infrastructure.

"Once we had the manpower in place, it was easier for us to continue our growth," DeLuca says. "Since then, we have added as many as 1,000 stores a year. My long-term goal is to reach 10,000, but I learned from experience that we need to take our time getting there. We don't need to accelerate too fast, so we identified limits for sensible growth. Currently, we have 8,650 franchises around the world."

REMEMBER

252. Growth costs money. When your company begins to grow, to manage your cash flow you'll need good financial planning.
253. There are two types of growth—planned and unplanned.
254. Putting together a board of advisers or directors in the beginning of your business will help you to prepare for difficult transition periods.
255. Encourage your employees to learn and grow by taking advanced business classes. You may even choose to hire a consultant to help train employees for greater responsibilities.
256. If an employee is unable to or doesn't want to take on new challenges, then it is your responsibility to hire a new person to take over the job.
257. Hire above the level you really need so an employee can handle the job's responsibilities after the company has grown.
258. Design an organizational chart that includes empty slots above the positions for the people you have hired. Then employees will not be offended or surprised when you hire new people.
259. You will find that a business is easier when it is small and problems get bigger as the company grows.
260. When your company expands, be realistic about your expectations.
261. Sometimes a company makes more money with lower sales than it does when sales are higher.

CHAPTER 42

It Takes Different Talents for Different Stages of Growth

As your company grows, your job will change and you experience a difficult, but necessary transition. You'll have to accept many new responsibilities.

When a company is small, the owner is involved in every aspect of the business and is aware of everything that goes on. He or she has few employees, makes every decision and works closely with customers. But, as the business grows, the owner deals with many issues unrelated to his or her product or service—worker's compensation, employee guidelines and benefits, health insurance, perhaps even lawsuits. The owner has lost the ability to control detail and is very far removed from the daily operations of his or her business.

Letting go

You must be certain you're willing to evolve with your business. No longer will you be able to do the same things you used to enjoy—

you will be an administrator. "Jane," an entrepreneur who owns a large chain of interior decorating studios, made the wrong choice when she expanded her business. When the business was small, she was very happy working with her customers in their homes and her office. The business grew and Jane now owns dozens of locations. Now, she spends her days negotiating leases for new stores with attorneys and real estate brokers. She is miserable.

You will have to let go of old responsibilities for new ones when you expand your business. No matter what your product or service is, your responsibilities will change as your business grows. If hands-on work is your passion, don't expand your business. There's nothing wrong with keeping a business small. The choice is yours.

When I started California Closets, I spent most of my time with customers and installing closets. As the business grew, I had to spend my time selling closets and hiring installers—and eventually salespeople. When I franchised, I was forced to hire a management team, so I could spend my time with attorneys and bankers. Eventually, I was completely removed from my customers. So, I made a greater effort to continue direct contact with my customers. By doing so, I was able to keep tabs on my business and their satisfaction.

Preparing for the change

Be prepared for new responsibilities. I prepared myself by asking my mentors for help. I went to my mentors—established business people—and asked them how to handle my new responsibilities. I asked many questions about what I should expect as my business grew, and they prepared me. I was very grateful for their assistance.

Subway's development

Fred DeLuca saw his company, Subway, grow from a one-store business to 8,000 restaurants around the world. His responsibilities have changed a lot since the days he was making the sandwiches himself.

"My role now is to provide guidance and leadership," DeLuca explains.

Once Subway entered the world of franchising, DeLuca discovered every time a decision was made, he heard complaints. "There were many complaints from my franchisees about our advertising campaigns," the founder explains. "It became necessary to delegate this responsibility to them. The franchisees devised a system where they elect a board of directors who make every advertising decision. This is a democratic approach and it gets the job done!"

DeLuca recalls it was necessary to delegate responsibility and authority once his business grew. "If you are an authoritarian, you will have to change your management style," he says. "This style won't work when your company becomes a large organization. Instead, you must get things done through persuasion.

"Every employee must understand that the direction of the company is a good one," DeLuca continues. "Each employee has to understand his or her role to be motivated to pitch in. I am the leader. It's my responsibility to persuade my people to go in a certain direction."

DeLuca understands that decisions are not as easy to make and implement when a business grows to an immense size. "It is more difficult to make changes now that I have department heads responsible for their own areas," he reveals. "I can't change anything without their input and approval. It takes forever to make a change because so many people are involved in the process now.

"As my business evolved, so did I!" he exclaims.

REMEMBER

262. As your company grows, your job will change and you'll experience a difficult, but necessary transition.
263. Let go of old responsibilities for new ones when you expand your business.
264. Be prepared to accept new responsibilities.
265. If hands-on work is your passion, don't expand your business. There's nothing wrong with keeping a business small.
266. Make an effort to continue direct contact with your customers. By doing so, you'll be able to keep tabs on your business and their satisfaction.

CHAPTER 43

The Winds of Change

The worst kind of entrepreneur is one who says, "This is the way my business has always been. We don't need to change anything." This president doesn't realize his or her business must change just to survive in today's competitive market. If the company fails to explore new methods, procedures and technology, it will fall far behind every competitor.

We live in a competitive world—the strong survive, and the weak go out of business. No business that is reluctant to change can compete effectively. It is necessary to take certain risks—be unique and different and not afraid to change. If a company refuses to change, competitors will control the market. To maintain and increase a customer base, you have to constantly look for new and better ways to do things.

The worst thing a business owner can say is: "I won't fix it if it's not broken." Regardless of whether a company needs repair, it still needs to improve and find new and unique ways to operate. To grow, a business must be flexible, adaptable and willing to create change. A business must be on the leading edge of technology to succeed. If your business does not find new and innovative ways to serve the customer—your business moves backward—while the competition will move ahead, leaving your company in the dust.

Resources for new ideas

You have two very valuable resources that can provide you with many new and innovative ways to run your business—your customers and your employees. I discovered many of my best concepts by asking customers how my company could improve. I merely asked and listened.

Your employees can be a valuable source of information. Ask them how your business can better serve the needs of the customer. While considering a specific change, involve your employees and ask for their input—don't force sudden change on them.

REMEMBER

267. No business that is reluctant to change can compete effectively.
268. Take risks and don't be afraid to change.
269. Maintain and increase a customer base, by seeking new and better ways to do what you do.
270. Improve and find new and unique ways to operate.
271. Employees and customers are two valuable resources that can suggest innovative ways to run your business.

CHAPTER 44

A Lifetime Education Program

When people ask me where I went to school, they expect me to name a prestigious Ivy League school or well-known MBA program. Well, I didn't attend Harvard or Stanford—in fact, I just barely graduated from high school! But the school I did attend was the school of hard knocks and I graduated from there with honors! I was a student of building and learning how to manage and operate my successful business. Because I learned the hard way, I can offer sound advice.

Looking back, it would have been useful to learn about the theoretical end of owning a business from a business school. But, since it isn't possible to learn the real nuts and bolts of starting and owning a business in a classroom, I wouldn't trade my self-taught education for any degree. Hard knocks taught me more than any school.

Whether you graduated from *my* alma mater or earned an MBA from one of the more prestigious business schools, your education must continue throughout your entire career. Too many business owners believe once their business has grown, they know everything. They stop trying to learn, and eventually stagnate. Always broaden your knowledge by trying to improve your product or service, In other words, keep growing!

Being flexible

From time to time, you may catch yourself saying, "This is the way it has always been done." When a business owner digs his or her heels into the ground, that business can't be flexible and adapt to the ever-changing world. Not good! A business continues to fulfill needs for the customer by discovering new and better ways to serve the customer, while staying ahead of the competition.

As the business owner, you must stay on the forefront of your industry regardless of the product or service your company offers. Resist the comforts of familiarity. Seek positive changes to incorporate into your business. Don't just reluctantly adapt to a changing market—constantly search for changes and welcome them into your business plan.

Learning by association

Your active involvement with any peer group can be very helpful, not just for the networking we discussed earlier, but to learn what's going on in your industry. Meeting with business owners, you learn marketing trends and ways to improve your manufacturing and sales processes. I met dozens of entrepreneurs through my involvement with Young Entrepreneur's Organization. Some of my colleagues were not in the industry, yet I learned from them, too. That invaluable advice from other entrepreneurs gave California Closets a big boost!

Adult education classes

Every entrepreneur can benefit from a basic course in accounting. You don't have to become an accountant, but you should be able to read and understand a balance sheet, a profit and loss statement, and a cash flow statement.

When I first started, I didn't know the difference between a general ledger and a profit and loss statement. I didn't even know how to balance my checkbook! This is why I decided to learn the basic principles of accounting. I went to night school in accounting, as well as other areas in which I needed to expand my knowledge, such as marketing and law. I felt it was important for me to understand my employees and consultants and I was right. Of course, you can hire all the specialists you need to help your business, but it certainly doesn't hurt to understand what they tell you! As the owner, you should have a basic understanding of every aspect of your business.

Doing your homework

Remember what it was like when you were in school? You spent the entire day in class, and then went home and did your homework. Well, owning a business is not unlike that. If you spent all of your time concentrating on nothing but your business, you'd lose touch with your competition, customers and the industry as a whole.

This is why I recommend reading trade magazines, taking classes, attending conferences and becoming involved with associations. You should do all you can to learn about your chosen field. I used a clipping service. Every three to four months, they provided me with a collection of newspaper and magazine clippings—stories and advertisements related to the closet industry. I kept abreast of my competition and general marketplace.

Learning from your customers

Your customers are your best critics. They know what they want, so don't hesitate to ask them! You can do this by organizing a customer focus group. Invite 15 or 20 former and present customers to an informal meeting. You can schedule a weeknight and serve dinner—most people would be happy to come under these conditions. Once you have the group together, ask for their opinions and input on how you can improve your products and customer service.

Don't be afraid to hear criticism—you learn a lot by listening to it. The owners of most companies don't want to hear about the problems. They feel they are being attacked by the customer. Place yourself above this attitude and listen to the constructive criticism.

REMEMBER

272. There is no excuse for you to not be an expert in your business if you continue learning.
273. A business continues to fulfill needs by discovering new and better ways to serve the customer and stay ahead of competition.
274. A business owner must remain on the forefront of industry regardless of the product or service.
275. Resist the comforts of familiarity. Be the innovative company that leads the market changes.
276. An active involvement with your peer group teaches you what is going on in your company's industry. Other business owners can inform you about marketing trends and ways to improve manufacturing and sales.
277. Take classes in unfamiliar areas such as marketing and law. As a business owner, you need a basic understanding of every aspect of your business.
278. Read trade magazines to learn all you can about your chosen field.
279. Customers are your best critics. Organize a customer focus group of 15 or 20 former and present customers.
280. Don't be afraid to hear criticism—instead, learn by listening to it.

CHAPTER 45

Long-Term Thinking and Planning

Your business operates day-to-day. But for it to be successful, you must be a good planner and a visionary who thinks year-to-year.

Every business has a strategy, whether the owner knows it or not! Ideally, you will define this strategy, setting goals realistic for your business—ones you expect to reach within a reasonable time. This keeps you focused, and informs your employees where the business is headed.

Since change is inevitable, as your company develops, you will replan and rethink your goals. As you add new goals to your list, you'll drop others that have become obsolete. New circumstances will affect your long-term plans, so don't narrow-mindedly set your goals in stone.

Involve your key employees in helping create long-term plans— after all, they will be doing most of the work. Once you establish your goals, clearly communicate them to your employees. Employees who are aware of company goals can help the company reach them, if they understand where the business is going and why it is important to get there.

227

You may want input from outsiders when developing your long-term plan. Consider using consultants or advisers who are experienced in your industry.

Once you have developed, refined and polished your long-term plan, write it down. This legitimizes the plan and facilitates the process of effectively communicating it to your management, employees, investors and anyone else who can help you achieve the goals.

The business environment, your market and your products will all change. Strategies and plans must adapt to an ever-changing business environment. So you will have to reevaluate and rethink your business plan on a yearly basis and allow it to evolve, too.

Successful entrepreneurs respond to change in a positive manner, coming up with new plans quickly. Entrepreneurs understand there is always more than one way to reach a goal. They devise multiple strategies, to avoid limiting themselves when one method fails.

Subway's long-term thinking and planning

In 1982, there were 200 Subway sandwich stores around the United States. Founder and CEO Fred DeLuca examined the development of other fast-food chains and realized a new goal after 17 years in business.

"At that time, all of the hamburger restaurants, such as McDonald's, had rapidly increased in size," he says. "My company had done a great job of growing from one store to 200, and had a lot of experience in operations and franchising. I was sure it was time to rethink our company goals.

"I thought it was possible to have 5,000 stores in 12 years—by 1994. But when I formally announced the new goal to my employees at a company meeting, they had no response! I was very disappointed that they were not more excited—I thought they would cheer and applaud loudly. Instead, they were passive!

"That night, I asked my wife, Elizabeth, who was at the company meeting, what she thought of the speech. She thought this over carefully, and responded, 'They think you are crazy!'

" 'You have 200 stores,' she continued, 'and you want 4,800 more! That is a big difference.'

"Since it seemed simple to me, I decided to spend a lot of time convincing my people the goal was attainable.

"This was a turning point for Subway because it gave us a new direction to head for," the founder continues. "We didn't know exactly how we would reach the goal, but at least we knew the time frame and the objective. My employees knew when they went to work every day, their goal was to reach our objective.

"The 5,000-store goal created a lot of energy in the company," he says. "Every decision made thereafter was based on facilitating the achievement of this 5,000-store mark."

DeLuca enthused and motivated his employees by constantly reminding them of the goal. The goal of 5,000 stores was surpassed; today the company has more than 8,650 stores around the world.

REMEMBER

281. Your business operates day-to-day, but you must think year-to-year.
282. Goals should be realistic for your business and reachable within a reasonable time.
283. Involve key employees in creating long-term plans—after all, they will be doing most of the work.
284. Clearly communicate ideas and goals to employees. Employees who are aware of company goals can help the company reach them, but only if they understand where the business is going, why it is important to get there and what they can do to help.
285. Motivate employees by reminding them of the goals.
286. Get input from outsiders—consultants or your board of directors who are experienced in your industry—when developing your long-term plan.
287. Once you have developed, refined and polished your long-term plan, write it down.
288. Strategies and plans must be flexible and able to adapt to an ever-changing business environment.
289. Long-term planning also requires reevaluating your business plan on a yearly basis.
290. You must be able to respond to change in a positive manner, creating new plans very quickly. Devise multiple strategies, so you won't limit yourself if one method fails.
291. Make decisions that will help achieve your goals.
292. Goals that are short-sighted or unquantifiable goals can be detrimental to a business.

CHAPTER 46

The Franchise Advantage

Franchising has been very good to me; in fact, I sold my first California Closet franchise in 1982. But I didn't start my business with the idea of franchising it—no one should do that.

People often tell me they want to start a business so they can franchise it. I quickly advise them, "First, have a good business, then franchise it." Only when you're at a point where you feel successful enough to bring others into your business, should you consider franchising.

How franchising works

If your business has a product or service that can easily be duplicated and made profitable in other locations, you may be able to franchise it. When you sell a franchise, you sell to others the right to duplicate your business and use your name, logo and trademark. In exchange for an upfront fee, ongoing royalty payments, and possible advertising contributions, you will provide to your franchisees guidance, support, marketing and advertising, and, in some cases, assistance in securing financing.

Expansion through franchising

Franchising is one of the best methods to expand a business. When a business is young, it's not practical to attempt to expand quickly with company-owned stores, as the margin is nominal and the expenses high. Through franchising, a company receives upfront money paid by franchisees that can be used for expansion. This beats having to find investors to raise needed capital.

Burt Cohen, vice president of licensing for McDonald's Corporation, believes the company's success as a system is due, to a large extent, to the franchises. "We do have the capability to run and control the whole U.S. system ourselves if we converted all our restaurants to company-operated, but we couldn't do as good a job as the franchisees. We have always been committed to franchising as a way of doing business," adds Cohen. "Eighty-two percent of our domestic restaurants are owned by franchisees, and we are franchising in each of our major foreign markets."

"If you find a true entrepreneur or someone who understands the concept of risk and reward; someone who has his or her money on the line, with the family's future at stake, he or she will always do a better job than a salaried employee," the senior vice president of licensing explains.

According to the company's licensing department, McDonald's receives over 20,000 inquiries a year for franchises. "We interview about 2,000 people and place 150 to 200," adds vice president Cohen. "We require a training program that takes about two years on a part-time basis—about 15 to 20 hours a week. We encourage people to train part-time so they are able to change their minds at any time while we can do the same without putting a financial strain on them and their families."

CENTURY 21® International

Signing up the first CENTURY 21, real estate services franchisees may have been the most difficult sales job of all time. The company's founder, Art Bartlett, vividly recalls those early days back in 1971:

"You can just imagine the reaction we got when we'd ask a real estate broker for $500 to become a franchisee of the CENTURY 21 system. The prospect would look at us like we were crazy and say, 'Now, let me get this straight. I've been in business for 30 years, and this business belonged to my father before me. We're known throughout the entire community. And what you want me to do is this: You want me to take my name off the sign and put up your brand-new name that's unknown, and you want me to pay you $500 to do that? Then, I have to pay you 6 percent on my gross revenue for the rest of my life? You know, Art, you've been out to a long lunch!' "

In what seemed an impossible task, Bartlett and his partner Marshall Fischer did convince real estate brokers to sign up, making the CENTURY 21 system the largest real estate franchisor in the world.

In return for being part of the CENTURY 21 system, franchisees benefit from the powerful image the company has created through its extensive advertising and marketing campaigns. Being part of the system offers a company name that has been pre-sold to the public, creating consumer preference. Additionally, the CENTURY 21 system provides its franchisees and their employees with sales training programs and training materials—something they may not be able to afford as an independent.

CENTURY 21 system franchisees must participate in the day-to-day business of their operation. In addition, franchisees must maintain the CENTURY 21 system's ethical and customer service standards. Strict guidelines proscribe the use of the CENTURY 21 system trademark and logo, yet franchisees are allowed to operate autonomously. Franchisees are offered as little or as much service as they want.

By franchising the CENTURY 21 system, Bartlett turned his small business into a booming enterprise. No other real estate network in the world handles more real estate transactions, has more offices or more sales associates, or is represented in more cities and communities than the CENTURY 21 system. This incredible growth occurred within a short period of time. Currently, CENTURY 21 system brokers and sales associates assist over 800,000 families to buy or sell properties each year. This translates into an estimated $80 billion in real estate sold worldwide, with approximately $2.2 billion in commissions.

Why PIP franchised

Bill LeVine, founder of PIP quick-printing company, was a pioneer in franchising. Yet, according to the entrepreneur, he was not initially interested in franchising his business, but merely expanding his business. "In 1966, a salesman named Bill Hensley called on me at my office and tried to convinced me that my business was franchisable," he recalls. "At the time, I didn't believe in the concept of franchising! But to get rid of him, I agreed to open a booth at a business opportunity show in Los Angeles. I put one of our cameras in it. You can imagine my surprise when I quickly sold three franchises! I wasn't even serious about selling a franchise—it was an easy sale! I immediately hired Hensley to be my franchise sales manager!

"The first franchise, opened in Whittier, California, in 1967, is still operating," he says.

"Though I had not made a conscious decision to pursue franchising, once I saw what could happen, I knew franchising was great. Franchising my concept was easy for the first five years," he continues. "In 1969, we sold 69 franchises and almost killed ourselves because we couldn't take care of that many! We didn't have the infrastructure to support the new units. It took a while, but we managed because by the time I sold the company in January 1988, I had 1,120 locations in the U.S., Canada and England."

According to LeVine, PIP offers many benefits to franchisees. "We taught the business to our franchisees, while an independent is out on his or her own. We helped our franchisees put everything together and get their business off the ground. We also provided knowledge, advertising and marketing.

"Throughout the years, we had very few problems with our franchisees," he says. "The relationship I had with my franchisees was that of a partnership. I bent over backwards to avoid conflict with my franchisees. If a franchisee was unhappy, we helped him or her sell the unit—we didn't turn it into a big issue. Companies who sell a franchise only to make money off the initial fees don't understand what the franchisor-franchisee relationship is all about, and they are the ones who have problems."

How Pizza Hut franchised

Frank Carney, co-founder of Pizza Hut, admits that he and his brother Dan pursued franchising as a method for expansion. "In the beginning, we sold the earliest franchises to anybody who had capital and desire—the two main ingredients."

Although they did reject a handful of applicants, they were willing to gamble on almost anyone who was willing to help them expand their restaurant concept around the country. The Carneys charged low franchise fees and confess they did not make a profit from franchising for several years.

"Our original agreement with one of our earliest franchisees, who is still with the system, required him to pay no more than $50 a month in royalty fees," recalls Carney. "If he didn't earn that much, then the he didn't have to pay it."

Many of the Carneys' earliest franchise agreements were actually written down on napkins and cemented by a handshake The company continued to operate in this casual manner for its first 10 years of existence.

Dan and Frank Carney chose not to sell franchises one unit at a time, but instead sold regions. "We decided early on that if someone is going to own one store in a city, they had better own them all, and if they don't want to own more than one store, then perhaps they ought to go to a small town that is only going to need one unit. We didn't want our franchises to be competing with each other. We always thought of cities as individual markets," says Frank Carney.

Under the auspices of Frank Carney, the company expanded at an accelerated rate. The entire country was sold by 1972, region by region, to a number of franchises while Pizza Hut retained various territories to operate as company-owned. During the first five years of existence, the company grew to more than 50 stores. By 1976, 18 years after the first restaurant opened, Pizza Hut had over 2,000 stores. Currently, the restaurant has over 9,500 units around the world, more than half of which are franchises.

The disadvantages of franchising

Although franchising is a quick way to expand nationally with minimal personal investment, there's a downside. When you franchise your business, you lose some control—and you have to deal with franchisees, who can be independent and demanding.

The most significant disadvantage to franchising a business is you won't be the owner of these franchised units. Unless you sign up competent franchisees, you cannot maintain the quality you want. Quality control is essential for a business to prosper. A successful franchised operation must meet standards of quality for products, customer service, cleanliness and store presentation, established by the corporate office. Every franchise must be uniform, providing customers with the standards they expect. Unfortunately, this is not always the case.

"If five people keep dirty stores and produce greasy products," says Bill Rosenberg, founder of Dunkin' Donuts, "this is a poor reflection on our entire system. If they are overlooked, our other franchisees will complain, 'I bought into this name, and it is not fair that a few poor stores are destroying business for the rest of us.' A few bad apples can hurt everyone's business. We must maintain the power to control all our franchisees in a positive direction; otherwise, our name means nothing. We are all in business for the same reason—to satisfy the customer. If certain people are doing something wrong, word spreads that we operate a bad chain. This hurts everybody in the company, many of whom have their life savings invested."

There are many more advantages than disadvantages to franchising a business. To maintain the standards you want, select your franchisees carefully.

Buying a franchise

On the other side of the coin, if you're someone who would like to own a small business but has limited experience or capital, investigate *buying* a franchise. Foremost, you will own a business that is already established, has name recognition, and a proven system that works.

Secondly, your franchisor is a resource who will help you solve every problem your business experiences.

These advantages are powerful. The Department of Commerce reports less than 5 percent of franchised outlets have failed or have been discontinued each year since 1971. For example, in 1989, less than 3 percent of new franchises were discontinued. In comparison, the U.S. Small Business Administration reports 65 percent of start-up businesses fail within the first five years.

In effect, purchasing a franchise is buying an insurance policy practically guaranteeing success. It's similar to paying a small premium—a *royalty*—that permits you to follow a proven success formula developed by the franchisor. While the franchise fee is an added cost, a good franchisor more than makes up for it by providing many benefits, such as economy-of-scale purchasing, national advertising, training, etc. Of course, many exceptional franchisors have wonderful national reputations that help you attract customers.

Investigate before you invest

Before you buy a franchise, thoroughly investigate the franchisor. One way to investigate is to visit and interview existing and former franchisees. Ask them if they had to do it all over, would they buy a franchise again? Don't be timid about asking questions—this is the best way to learn the positives and the negatives. You may even want to spend a few days or weeks working in a location. After all, you should be sure you will enjoy and understand what the company does. You should also believe in the product or service.

Next, examine the franchisor's track record. Is the company financially stable or is it relying on franchise fees to keep going? What is the failure, turnover or termination rate of its franchisees? Does the company assist its franchisees when searching for a location? What training programs does the company offer? Does the company have good communication with its franchisees? Does it allow its franchisees to have input in decision-making? And how are advertising dollars spent?

Finally, you should read the company's Uniform Franchise Offering Circular (UFOC). Every franchisor is required by the U.S. Federal

Trade Commission to complete this 23-section form, which details its franchisees, and any pending or past litigation that involved the company. The UFOC also includes a forecast of franchisees' earnings, costs and payments plus an explanation of how the franchisor advertises (including money spent, type of media used and extent of coverage).

In the UFOC, franchisors must identify training programs they offer (including subject matter and time frame), the table of contents from the franchise operating manual and instructions for operating the franchise. Financing arrangements are disclosed in detail in addition to the franchisor's financial interests in any purchases they require of franchisees.

The federal government requires every franchisor to supply this information to every qualified candidate who applies for a franchise. Don't buy a franchise before reading this document!

Advantages for franchisees

Some franchisors offer more services than others. A secret to McDonald's success lies in the meticulous operating procedures for food preparation and service provided by the franchisor to its licensees. A 750-page operations-and-training manual given to each licensee provides specifics on how to run a McDonald's restaurant successfully. The manual spells out all details relating to the chain's fundamentals of quality, service, cleanliness and value, reminding operators that hamburgers and french fries must be thrown out 10 minutes after they are made if not sold, and windows must be washed every day.

Pizza Hut franchisees have the option of purchasing supplies through PepsiCo Food Service. Over 99 percent of the system's franchisees use PFS for one-stop shopping, where they can purchase everything needed to operate their unit(s), from tomatoes to pepperoni. Franchisee Bill Walsh believes the royalties paid to Pizza Hut are justified by purchasing power enjoyed by the franchisees. "We save more money on the cost of goods we purchase as a group than we pay out as a royalty," he says.

Former Pizza Hut CEO Steve Reinemund, believes team performance is critical and there are no winners on a losing team and no losers on a winning team.

"I think franchisees are only as successful as the parent company, and the parent company is only as successful as the franchisees."

A good franchisor is one that has a balanced relationship with its franchisees. The best franchisors allow their franchisees to have input in most major decisions. Pizza Hut marketing vice president Bob Perkins explains, "The franchisees' input belongs in everything we do. Since the average franchisees have been in the system for about 13 years, I can count on them as a tremendous source of new ideas, advice, input, guidance and counsel. The franchises are the backbone of this system— particularly from a historical perspective. We meet with them quarterly and, believe me, we do a lot of listening when they speak!"

My mother and former vice president of franchise relations for California Closets, Roberta Balter, agrees: "To understand where your franchisees are coming from, you have to listen very carefully—not just to the words, but to their intent.

"A franchisor who listens carefully, observes and understands its franchisees' needs and what they are trying to accomplish, will be able to help them achieve success.

"My role as the vice president of franchise relations was to help people achieve their dreams," she adds. "I did this through the art of listening and understanding what our franchisees really wanted.

"The most important thing is to helping people achieve their dreams," Balter explains. "This is what franchising is all about."

Unrealistic expectations

Many franchisees have been crushed by their unrealistic expectations. If you expect to make more money than you know what to do with, you set the scene for disappointment. In return for a small royalty you'll pay as long as you own the franchise, your franchisor will provide a proven success method. Don't expect to make millions of dollars selling pizzas, submarine sandwiches or even closets! Very few people earn an enormous amount of money by owning a franchised business. When you purchase a franchise, you're buying yourself a job, not a quick buck. In the past, a franchisee who started out with one McDonald's unit may have ended up with 50, earning over $2 million every year, but this isn't typical. Most franchisees own one or two units and take home $50,000 to $100,000 each year. This is a comfortable living, but demands hard work. On the bright side, you can't be fired or laid off!

REMEMBER

293. Franchising is one of the best methods to expand a business.
294. Although franchising is a quick way to expand nationally with minimal personal investment, don't start a business to franchise it.
295. It is more difficult to manage and standardize the quality, products, service, cleanliness and store presentation at franchised units than company-owned units.
296. Choose your franchisees carefully.
297. When you franchise your business, you lose some control—and you have to deal with franchisees, who can be independent and demanding.
298. A successful franchised operation must meet standards of quality for products, customer service, cleanliness and store presentation, established by the corporate office.
299. Every franchise must be uniform, providing customers with the standards they expect.
300. Investigate before investing in a franchise.
301. Some advantages of owning a franchise are that it is an already established business, has name recognition, and a proven system that works. A franchisor is a resource who will help you solve every problem your business experiences.
302. Less than 5 percent of franchised outlets have failed or have been discontinued each year since 1971.
303. Don't expect to make millions of dollars as a franchisee, but you'll make a great living and you'll be the boss!

CHAPTER 47

Creating an Image That Suits Your Company

When you begin a new business, you may compete for customers alongside established businesses that have proven track records. Your company may have the disadvantage of being unknown in the marketplace. To compete, your company needs an image—one that is carefully conceived.

It is better to start out with no image at all and begin building one slowly than it is to allow the wrong image to develop and later be unhappy with it. It is much easier to build a new image than to change an undesirable one. An image will evolve whether you want it to or not! But don't wait for an image to develop automatically. Consciously develop it in order to end up with the one you really want.

Unless a target niche has been identified, it is next to impossible to create an image that suits your company. Once the needs, desires and personality of your market are understood, you can begin to develop an effective image that will appeal to those future customers.

Creating an image

Your company's image is based on your targeted market. A small company cannot be everything to everybody—only corporations such as Ford Motor Company or Coca-Cola can attempt to encompass a large market. A small clothing store, for example, can't have a line of clothing for men, women and children and offer high-end and discounted merchandise—only a large department store may be able to do this. A small store must decide what kind of operation it wants to be, then gear itself toward that market.

It is possible to vary your company's image by appealing to different types of customers. This is accomplished through separate marketing campaigns or repackaging the product altogether. McDonald's did this with its hamburger, drink and french fries. These products are not only listed on the regular menu, but also as part of a special package called a "Happy Meal"—a product that is marketed to children. Here, they are marketing the same products to children and adults through two different campaigns.

Every consumer wants the best value for the dollar. To varying degrees, consumers evaluate price point, quality and service before making a purchase. But, a high-end consumer will pay more for better service and higher quality, while a lower-end market sacrifices quality for the least expensive price. An image must be created to attract the interest of the consumers targeted.

California Closet's image

My company was the most expensive around. No other offered the same level of quality and service, and my customers were willing to pay more for our services. Our competition was able to offer closets for less money by using lower quality materials. California Closets portrayed an image to attract high-end buyers willing to pay more for the best product.

Your company should zero in on its market. If you sell to middle America, you shouldn't have snob-appeal. We portrayed a very professional image to appeal to our executive customers. My representatives were required to wear professional clothing when meeting with customers, and every representative of my company had to be on time for an appointment—from salespeople to installers—this attitude was carried through the whole process.

Customer expectations

A customer's perception of a company is influenced by his or her expectations. Exceeding a customer's expectations is an excellent way to boost your company's image. Customers expect a certain level of service, quality and value; giving them more than that will delight them.

H & R Block's image

Tax preparer H & R Block purposely portrays itself as a local company. To accomplish this, it feeds commercials directly to local television stations for airing, rather than pursuing national network advertising.

"Many people think we are local," Richard Bloch, co-founder, explains. "In the beginning, no one had any idea we were anywhere but local, and that was the impression we wanted to give.

"Even though we have TV ads running in most major markets, customers still believe we live in their hometowns of Milwaukee, Toledo, or Sacramento."

H & R Block discovered that consumers prefer a local, friendly entity doing their tax work, over a large, faceless corporation. Block commercials stress quality tax preparation, peace of mind, and the company's ability to help taxpayers get the biggest refund they're entitled to. Company spokesperson Henry Bloch, Richard's brother and co-founder, appears in nearly every advertisement. Henry's distinguished appearance and straightforward honesty is perceived by the public to reflect a sincere image—precisely what the company needs to attract customers. It is not uncommon for them to a call an H & R Block office asking for Henry to do their tax work personally!

Richard Bloch believes H & R Block commercials adequately reveal the company's principles and the image it wants to portray. "Our principles are straightforward," he says. "I really believe that we do the finest possible work and charge fairly. We stand behind our work. And believe me, these principles are just as important and true today to our customers as they were 30 years ago."

REMEMBER

304. Don't wait for an image to develop automatically.
305. To compete, your company needs a carefully conceptualized image.
306. Once the needs, desires and personality of your market are understood, you can develop an effective image to appeal to your future customers.
307. It is better to start out with no image at all and begin building one slowly than to allow the wrong image to develop and later be unhappy with it.
308. It is possible to vary your company's image by appealing to different types of customers through separate marketing campaigns and repackaging the product.

CHAPTER 48

The Stability Image

In all facets of life, a stable image can greatly affect your relationship with others. As a business owner, a stable image is especially important. People are concerned about your company's longevity and long-term success. They need to know your relationship with them is durable. A flash-in-the-pan image scares people away. You want to build a stable image for your customers, employees, business associates and yourself.

Ways to project a stable image

Financial institutions realized the importance of a stable image long ago. Why does every leading bank construct a giant edifice to house its offices? To established stability in the minds of its customers—for what is more permanent than a solidly constructed office building? That certain "bank look" conveys permanency. People who trust their lifetime savings to a bank want to believe that the institution will "live forever."

The same holds true for every type of business, regardless of the product. An impressive location that gives customers a sense of security is useful when building solid business relationships. Naturally, the "right" piece of real estate is a worthwhile investment.

Because its very nature is intangible, a service business has a greater need for a stable image. It needs something concrete that can be seen and touched—which its service can't provide. Owning a permanent fixture is more worthwhile for a service type of business than businesses that have fixed assets in their equipment or carry large inventories.

Not every business needs or can afford to own a structure to convey the message of stability. Projecting a stable image doesn't always require real estate. A less expensive way is the quality of your marketing materials. Nothing gives a company a weaker image than a handmade or makeshift sales kit. Without a first-class sales aid, prospective clientele suspect your company lacks both professionalism and money, or assume you are new in your field. This poor image will decrease your company's chances of achieving a share of the marketplace.

McDonald's uses a simple technique to remind its customers of its longevity and stability. At every restaurant, beneath the McDonald's name on the large sign in front, there is a simple phrase that says it all— "Billions and Billions Sold." What does this mean to a customer? McDonald's is saying "We have been around forever, and we are going to be here for a long time." People look for stability. This is the reason California Closets representatives tell customers how many years we have in business and how many closets we have remodeled. The numbers say it all.

Customer confidence

Customers want to feel the company they do business with will be around for a long time. If your business is not doing well, never let the customer know! Never tell a customer anything about your business that isn't totally positive. Otherwise, they might lose confidence in you. Tell every customer that business is great, even if it isn't. Customers don't want to use a company they think may not be in business down the road. Why do people shop at Sears? Because it is stable and predictable. If they have a problem with a Sears product they know it can be serviced or returned. After they buy, customers feel the salespeople will be around for service. It is more difficult for new or smaller businesses to gain customer confidence, yet these are the companies that need it the most. Once a company proves it is stable, it gains customer confidence.

REMEMBER

309. A stable image is necessary to gain the support and confidence of your customers, employees and business associates.
310. Use of professional quality marketing materials projects a stable image.
311. Customers want to feel your company will be around for a long time.
312. If business is bad, never let a customer know!
313. Once you prove your company is stable, you gain customer confidence.

CHAPTER 49

The Credibility Image

At one time or another, all of us have experienced the frustration of an unfulfilled promise. Have you been disappointed when a tailor failed to have your suit or dress altered by a promised date? Remember when the contractor who assured you your home would be completed by May made you wait until December? How about when your car was to be repaired by Tuesday and it wasn't? We all have agonized over such broken promises. The company you deal with may produce a good product, but you forget this when it fails to meet a deadline. Every successful business must follow through with every promise made to a customer. Though it may seem elementary and reasonable, the pursuit of a credible image is not shared by many businesses.

Never disappoint a customer

It is better to give a customer more than expected than to disappoint by providing less. Many businesses stretch the facts when they project what they're going to do for a customer. How amazing these companies do not have the foresight to see how foolish they will appear when they fail to produce what they have promised. The failure to perform as promised gives a company a losing image, and you must avoid it like the plague.

Until proven wrong, customers innocently believe a business will follow through on its promise. The company that fails to meet a promise frustrates its customers, who may choose never to do business there again. Customers appreciate a professional who does what's promised. Even businesses with an outstanding product achieve only mediocre results if they lack the necessary follow-through. Conversely, a company with an inferior product will outperform the competition if it meets the customer's expectations on time. It doesn't matter how outstanding the end result may be; a customer who had to suffer unbearable frustration to get it will not feel he or she received good value.

Projecting a credible image

To project a credible image to your customer, employ the complete package of good marketing and customer service. You may have the best marketing in the world, but if your employees don't project a credible image; you're sunk. Employees on every level, from your receptionist to your salesperson, need to deal with customers in a professional manner to gain their trust and confidence.

Your employees should never inconvenience a customer. A receptionist alienates potential customers by putting them on hold for a long period of time. Salespeople do this when they show up late for an appointment. Customers rightly interpret this behavior as a disrespect for their time. When my company tells a customer he or she can count on us, we do it without fail, and according to schedule. Meeting a deadline must be top priority.

If you plan on a long and rewarding career, you'll be doing business with others over a long period of time. You must develop a credible image if you want a business to have the repeat customers and referrals your company needs to succeed.

REMEMBER

314. It is better to give a customer more than expected than to disappoint by providing less.
315. Businesses with an outstanding product achieve only mediocre results if they lack the necessary follow-through.
316. Customers do not feel they have received good value if they had to suffer unbearable frustration in the process.
317. Projecting a credible image to your customer is done through good marketing and employees who serve the customer.
318. Employees on every level, from your receptionist to your salesperson, need to deal with customers in a professional manner to gain their trust and confidence.

CHAPTER 50

The Image of Success

People want to deal with winners. Your customers have confidence in you and what you do when you project a winning image. The more successful your image, the more your customers want to do business with you. Every customer wants to feel good about doing business with a winning company, so take steps to ensure that your company has the image it needs.

Dressing for success

Because of its tremendous effect on your company, your image can be used to impress your customers. Since you want everything to go your way, you can't afford to wear clothes that might have an adverse effect on certain customers. If your shirt collar is frayed, your shoes not shined, your lapels out of style, or your tie uncleaned, you appear to be either unsuccessful or a slob! Either way, you lose!

The first impression you give is based on the way you dress. Why not present yourself in a professional manner when dealing with customers, suppliers and manufacturers? Depending on what you do and what part of the country you live in, there is a right way and a wrong way to dress. Sloppy or very casual dress may suggest you are flighty or capricious. Customers want to believe you will be around for a long time and give them service, and conservative dress signals this kind of stability.

A similar approach can be applied to your hair. Certainly, hair styles change from year to year. What was considered long hair in the '50s and early '60s is, by today's standards, quite conservative. The important thing to consider is neatness, rather than length. The same holds true for beards and mustaches. Neatly trimmed, they can give you a clean-cut look. Look at yourself carefully to see what image you portray to others.

Your self-image

Your good appearance and healthy self-image positively affect the way others see you. You project a winning image through your enthusiasm and the way you talk. The two most important impressions you make on a customer are the first one and the last one! When calling on a customer for the first time, get right down to business. Don't waste time talking weather, politics or false flattery. Such small talk suggests insecurity, and intrudes upon on a customer's time and privacy. It's much more effective to get to the point, and your customer will respect you for it. This is different from building a rapport with the customer.

Your company's image

Your company's image is based largely on its appearance. Once a place of business gets a reputation for dinginess, it's difficult to change. Whether you own a corner grocery, a fast-food burger operation or a lady's dress shop, bright lights, clean walls and shiny floors will give your business a good appearance!

Every retail store should strive for a clean look, because nobody wants to patronize a dirty-looking establishment, no matter how much quality is inside. Even a business operating on a small budget can afford fresh paint. If you can't afford a good janitorial service, roll up your sleeves and spend a few extra hours each week making sure dust doesn't accumulate on your shelves or products. A tidy appearance suggests you are efficient and well-organized—and there isn't a business that doesn't want this image. If you've ever walked into a service station that was neat and orderly, you undoubtedly felt more comfortable leaving your car there to be serviced.

Image shows in the way customers are treated by your employees, beginning with the first phone call. Have you ever called a company, received poor service from a receptionist, and hung up, never to try that business again? Sure, we all have. Low-paid receptionists are at the bottom of a company's totem pole. Yet, they have important responsibilities and a high degree of impact on the customer. When a receptionist treats a customer rudely, in that customer's mind she represents your entire company! Good companies train their receptionists to answer the telephone professionally. Each of my receptionists knows how to properly address callers, take information and answer questions. You can tell if someone is smiling by the way they speak, so I place a mirror on my receptionist's desk so she can see herself smile while talking to a customer!

Building an image through advertising

Your company can develop a successful image through advertising—it's a sometimes expensive but effective technique to build your company's image through television, radio, newspaper or magazines. One option that many companies are not aware of is the ability to advertise in a national, reputable newspaper or magazine on a regional basis. National publications such as *The Wall Street Journal, Business Week, Fortune, Time* and *Newsweek* have lower rates for advertisements that appear in issues distributed only in a particular section of the country. The average reader who reads such ads will believe your business is really booming. When advertising in this manner, however, be certain you don't pay for reaching a market so large you're incapable of serving it.

REMEMBER

319. Your appearance affects the image you create for your company.
320. Your company's image is based largely on appearance. Once a place of business gets a reputation for looking dingy, it's difficult to change.
321. Your company can develop a successful image through advertising—this can be expensive but effective. Don't pay for reaching a market so large you're incapable of serving it.

CHAPTER 51

Success Breeds Success

As the saying goes, nothing succeeds like success. But it is not enough simply to attract customers. Customers want to do business with companies that are winners—who have a successful image. To build a solid reputation, your company must create an image that breeds success.

Success-breeds-success techniques

The appearance of your office building, office decor and equipment are all part of your company's image. The extra expense to rent a luxurious high-rise, downtown office building rather than a one-floor, converted storeroom in the low-rent district, may be money well-spent. Depending on the business you're in, decorate your office with symbols that enhance your successful image—diplomas, academic certificates, plaques and awards tell your customers just how good you really are.

Why can many people in the arts demand such high prices for their work? An artist with a reputation for being expensive may have an easier time selling a painting than a more talented but unknown artist. I have seen artwork that looks like it was created in an hour, selling for three times an average annual salary! The secret is not talent, but the artist's ability to build a winning image.

Appear to be busy

Even when business is slow, your company should always appear busy. Never let clients know how few appointments you may have; instead, create the impression that you are booked solid. If a prospective customer is not available to see you at a certain time, say something like, "I'm sorry we can't meet on Tuesday at 8 a.m., but I can see you on Friday at 2:15 p.m. or next Monday at 9:30 a.m." You may not have any appointments for the next two months, but when you pull out your appointment book and busily look through it, your prospect gets the impression that he is fortunate indeed to be able to see you on the dates you suggest.

If the customer isn't available on any of the dates you suggested, but can meet Thursday at 2 p.m., offer to "juggle" your schedule to make room for him or her. You might say, "I am sure I can do some rearranging in order to see you then. Please be sure to mark it down on your own calendar because mine is very tight!" Although you are not saying it in these words, your message will be quite clear: I am very successful, and, therefore, I am very busy.

Appearing to be busy is even more important for smaller businesses. Some small firms purposely put their customers through a cross-examination before allowing them to speak with the boss. Only after customers go through a detailed explanation with the receptionist of who they are and why they are calling, are they transferred to the boss's private secretary. By the time the customer gets to speak with the boss, the boss is aware of exactly what information the customer needs. This is helpful for the customer as the boss may have an answer prepared in advance. It also creates an air of importance. If a business owner personally answers the phone, the customer may think business is slow or even bad.

Regardless of the manner in which you handle your telephone calls, customers should be treated in a professional manner. You never want a customer to feel he or she is being "put off." No caller should be given the runaround. Devise a plan for the calls your business receives—where the call will start (with a receptionist) to where the call will be routed according to the information requested.

The price is right

It's human nature to feel that the more you pay for services, the higher quality work you'll receive. Most customers will say, "At those prices, I've got the best that money can buy." There is much to be said in favor of equating quality with the price tag. For this reason, price your merchandise or services high enough so you don't scare customers away. Charging fees that are too low creates a negative image and may lessen your business. Raising your fees to the price that makes you look expensive suggests that you are also good.

REMEMBER

322. Everybody wants to be on a winning team, so project a successful image that attracts customers.
323. A company's office building, office decor and equipment are all part of its image.
324. Your company should appear busy even when business is slow.
325. Price your services or products high enough so you don't scare customers away. Charging fees that are too low can create a negative image.

CHAPTER 52

How to Generate Free Publicity

Advertising can be an expensive venture for a small business. It's tough on a tight budget to inform the public of your existence. An alternative way does exist and it is possible to obtain media coverage for your product without spending a fortune. Whether your budget is meager or unlimited, explore the alternative of promoting your company through public relations.

Newspapers, magazines, television shows and radio stations are constantly looking for new stories to cover. If your company offers a unique product or service, it's easy to convince an editor that a story about your company needs to be written. If your product is not unique, you can attract attention by creating an unusual promotional tactic. A public relations specialist is a professional trained to promote your product through creative use of the media. The exposure your company receives through good public relations is worth far more than you can ever imagine.

Be aware! If you are an advertiser with a certain magazine, newspaper, television or radio station, you're not entitled to receive coverage or publicity through that medium. First of all, advertising and editorial staffs do not have much contact with each other. Secondly, most producers and editors are highly ethical and opposed to covering a story about an advertiser because of pressure tactics. They will be much more likely to do a spread about your company or product if they are not made aware of the money you spend on advertising with them.

Public relations specialists

Hiring a public relations firm is a very worthwhile investment. Your company will generally receive more for its money from a public relations firm than through expensive advertising.

As the saying goes, advertising is cursed and public relations is blessed. People tend to believe what they read in an editorial format, while if the same information appeared in an advertisement, they would be much more skeptical. The same consumers who spurn ads consider journalistic endorsements credible sources of information!

Planning a presentation

To be featured on TV, radio or in a periodical is easier than you think. You just need to know how. Before approaching the media, pick a story idea about you or your product. Prepare a press kit containing a thoroughly planned presentation, and include photographs if possible. Editors and producers are sent dozens of press kits every week, so to stand out, yours should be different in some way. My press kit was always sent by overnight delivery—so it would have the appearance of being important—improving the chance it would be looked at.

Your presentation provides the producer or editor with a "hook" or an angle that will catch the attention of their audience. This "hook" can involve your background or how you created your service or product. If you don't have an interesting story to tell, create a promotional gimmick to attract attention, such as a contest.

Send your presentation to the editor of the section of the publication where your story would fit. The editor will decide if your story will be covered. If approved, it will be assigned to a writer. If it is rejected, change the angle of your story and submit it to another editor of a different section of the newspaper or magazine. Each TV and radio news show has a different producer for you to approach.

A good public relations specialist can create a campaign for even the most mundane product. You can be very creative. To attract publicity, my company had a messy closet contest. We also did many charity events. For example, if your business is a flower shop, donate day-old flowers to a convalescent home. This could be a great story for your local news show. Or, if your business is pool supplies and maintenance, you might donate free service to the local YMCA. The local media can turn this into a great story.

Pitching yourself or your product to media is not difficult. Editors, producers and reporters are eager for new stories to cover. Newspapers and magazines have many pages to fill up each day and are always in need of material—as are radio and television shows. An angle I used was to provide a service for their audience. Whenever I was on a news or talk show, I taught people 10 easy tips for organizing their closets that they could do themselves.

Before I appeared on Oprah Winfrey's show, my company organized her closets. Oprah was very happy with the results. During the show, she told the audience she loved her closets and that it was the best thing that ever happened to her! I was surprised to discover the tremendous affect being on Oprah had on my business. The month after the show ran was our best ever. We had more orders that month than in several months combined.

Oprah was also valuable for my company because she mentioned the name California Closets eight to 10 times during the hour-long show. And Oprah endorsed my product! What was the value of this publicity? Probably $1 million to my company. I reached my target market—a large part of my customer base watch her show. I was invited to be a guest on Oprah two more times. One reason I was invited back so many times was because I was very cooperative and professional with her staff. I sent thank-you notes and kept in touch with her producers.

I appeared on more than 200 television shows and in *The Wall Street Journal* and *People* magazine. The national exposure helped my company become successful. *The Wall Street Journal* put California Closets on the map overnight—sales of closets skyrocketed. So did franchise sales—we sold between 15 and 20 around the country because of the article. This one article was more valuable than all the advertising money we had spent to that point!

REMEMBER

326. Advertising is cursed and public relations is blessed. People believe what they read or hear in an editorial format, while they are skeptical of advertisements.
327. Prepare a press kit with a thoroughly planned presentation, and photographs if possible. It should include a "hook" or an angle to catch the attention of an audience.
328. Do not feel entitled to receive coverage or publicity if you are an advertiser. Advertising and editorial staffs do not have much contact.

CHAPTER 53

Home Office Tips

Thousands of successful businesses, including Hewlett-Packard, Apple Computer, Mrs. Smith's Apple Pies, Lillian Vernon and California Closets, share one thing in common. They were once operated out of a garage, attic, basement or on a kitchen table! Many companies now found in sprawling industrial complexes and towering skyscrapers were started in the homes of their founders.

Today, more than 40 million Americans work out of their homes in one capacity or another. Home offices are found not only in cramped spaces where every square foot is overfilled, but also in large rooms, replete with top-of-the-line technology. Some businesses that operate out of homes have full- or part-time employees who come in daily or hourly to perform specific tasks. Others are one-person enterprises that hire commissioned outside "reps," independent contractors and suppliers from all over the world.

Starting your new business at home has many advantages. The greatest one is that you won't have to lease space, which will keeps your overhead low. A second plus is flexibility and convenience; you can work around the clock, sleep when you want, and be close to your family.

Operating a successful business out of the home requires you to be a self-starter. Your office space must be free from interruptions, for it is very easy to be distracted. You must have the discipline to go into your office and shut the rest of the world out. It is essential for you to

267

have a separate space for your business, and an understanding with your family and friends that this is separate from the rest of the house.

Home offices are not for everybody

Many people can be happy and productive working at home while others cannot.

Ask yourself the following questions: Are you self-disciplined? Do you do what you must do each day without external pressure? Are you good at prioritizing tasks? Can you resist distractions? Do you enjoy working without a lot of people around? Do you like your home and being in it?

If you answered yes to each question, working at home may be for you. Certainly, it is not for everybody. Working out of the home can foster a sense of isolation and stagnation, create family problems and contribute to compulsive overwork. There are a few things you can do to maintain the health of your business and yourself. To make working at home a pleasant experience, take breaks away from your desk, exercise for a few minutes at odd times and establish a work routine that starts and stops so you don't burn yourself out.

Equipping your home office

In the last 10 years, technology dramatically changed the way people work, creating a home office revolution. Working out of the home is now a viable option for many. Before personal computers and faxes, only the President of the United States worked at home. In the 1990s, the home office is realistic and affordable for most any type of company.

Computers and other high-tech equipment designed exclusively for the home office can help even the smallest home businesses be competitive. In addition, sophisticated telephone technology, including voice mail, fax machines and modems, make sending, receiving and manipulating information easier than ever.

Leasing verses owning equipment

In the long term, buying new or used equipment is usually less expensive than leasing. It also does not necessitate the credit strength and history that leasing requires. Regardless of which you choose, you can deduct most business equipment expenses from your taxes.

There are a few advantages to leasing your equipment. Foremost, it improves your cash flow by tying up less operating capital than buying does. You can arrange terms and payments to fit the needs of your business. Some leases will permit you to change or upgrade the equipment as your company grows. If you choose to lease, then buy later, investigate open-end leases that allow you to purchase the equipment at the end of the lease period. Whether you buy or lease, be sure you understand exactly what's included for the price you will be paying.

Home office tax deductions

A business operating out of a home gains many tax deductions. Don't wait until tax time to make decisions that could lower your taxes. Ask your accountant whether buying or leasing equipment is more advantageous for your business. Keep your phone expenses separate by adding an additional line for your business use. The cost of installing and use of a second line is tax deductible if it is used exclusively for business purposes. Most importantly, organize your tax records and save them and all canceled checks for at least seven years. Discuss with an accountant and plan ahead. Tax planning should be a year-round endeavor.

REMEMBER

329. Operating a successful business out of the home requires you to be a self-starter.
330. Your office space must be free from interruptions.
331. Have the discipline to go into your office and shut the rest of the world out.
332. Take breaks away from your desk. Exercise.
333. Establish a routine so you don't burn yourself out.
334. Buying new or used equipment is usually less expensive than leasing.
335. Leasing your equipment ties up less operating capital, and it may permit you to change or upgrade the equipment as your company grows.
336. Think in terms of minimizing expenses to affect your company's overhead.
337. A business operating out of your home can take advantage of many tax deductions.

EPILOGUE

Hundreds of thousands of people have started new businesses since the early 1980s. Unfortunately, the statistics reported by the U.S. Small Business Administration are intimidating: An average of 65 percent of start-up businesses fail within the first five years. The reason why most new businesses fail is usually because of a lack of capital and poor management.

Don't let these statistics stop you from pursuing your dream of owning your own business. Undoubtedly, whether you have created a new concept or reinvented the wheel, you will experience many challenges. My hope is that the advice, tips and techniques you learned from this book will help you along the way.

Starting and building a business from the ground up is, perhaps, one of the most fulfilling accomplishments a person can achieve. It can be a terrific gamble, but it can also have a tremendous payoff. If I can do it, so can you.

Good luck!

SELECT RESOURCES

Breakaway Careers. Radin, Bill. Career Press.

Crafting the Successful Business Plan. Hyypia, Erik, and the editors at "Income Opportunities." Prentice-Hall.

How To Buy Advertising Like the Pros...and Save 15% to 50%. Brown, Marvin. Maarbro Guide.

How to Master the Art of Selling. 2d ed. Hopkins, Tom. Warner Books.

The Entrepreneur's Guide to Business Information. Lea, Jim. Career Press.

The Entrepreneur's Road Map to Business Success. Maul, Lyle, and Mayfield, Dianne. Saxtons River Publications.

Financing Your Small Business. Seglin, Jeffrey L. McGraw-Hill.

For Entrepreneurs Only. Harrell, Wilson. Career Press.

The Franchise Advantage. Borian, Donald D., and Borian, Patrick J. National BestSeller.

Franchise Opportunities. Sterling Publishing.

Franchising & Licensing: Two Ways to Build Your Business. Sherman, Andrew J. Amacom.

Franchising: The Business Strategy that Changed the World. Shook, Carrie, and Shook, Robert L. Prentice Hall.

The Great Game of Business. Stack, Jack. New York: Currency Books.

Guerrilla Marketing. Levinson, Jay C. Houghton Mifflin.

How to Run a Small Business. 5th ed. J.K. Lasser Tax Institute. Bernard Griesman, editor. McGraw-Hill.

The McGraw-Hill 36-Hour Accounting Course. Arnett, Harold E., and Dixon, Robert L. McGraw-Hill.

Men and Women at Work. Kearney, Katherine G. and White, Thomas. Career Press.

Power Networking. Vilas, Donna, and Vilas, Sandy. MountainHarbour.

The Small Business Handbook. Burstiner, Irving. Simon & Schuster.

The Smart Woman's Guide to Starting a Business. Montgomery, Vickie. Career Press.

The Service Edge. Zemke, Ron, and Shaaf, Dick. New York: New American Library.

Start Up, 3rd ed. Stolze, William J. Career Press.

Swim With the Sharks Without Being Eaten Alive. Mackay, Harvey. Ballantine Books.

What They Don't Teach You at Harvard Business School. McCormack, Mark H. Bantam Books.

Ziglar on Selling. Ziglar, Zig. Ballantine Books.

ABOUT THE AUTHORS

When Neil Balter's parents kicked him out of the house at 17 for having a "bad attitude," he resourcefully combined his carpentry skills with his entrepreneurial spirit and discovered a new market. Working out of a van, he transformed neighbors' messy closets into efficient, custom-designed storage areas. In his first year, he grossed almost $60,000. And so the California Closet Company was born.

In just over a decade, the company expanded to more than 100 franchises throughout the United States, Canada, Australia, Japan, New Zealand and Spain, with annual worldwide sales in excess of $70 million. In 1990, before his 30th birthday, Balter sold the company to Williams-Sonoma, Inc. Thus, closing the closet doors, he decided to take time out to write this book.

Balter is a founding member of the Young Entrepreneurs' Organization, an international group whose primary goals are education, business development and personal and entrepreneurial growth. As YEO president in 1992, he met with President George Bush to discuss issues of concern to small and medium-sized businesses.

Balter speaks frequently to audiences nationwide on a variety of topics, such as "What It Takes to be a Millionaire Before 30." He is the recipient of numerous prestigious professional honors including the *Entrepreneur Magazine* Outstanding Entrepreneur Achievement Award. From *The Wall Street Journal* and *Forbes,* to *People* magazine and "The Oprah Winfrey Show," more than 500 newspapers, magazines and TV shows have chronicled the inspirational story of Neil Balter.

Carrie Shook is a full-time author and journalist who resides in Columbus, Ohio. She has written six books including *Franchising—The Business Strategy That Changed the World* (Prentice-Hall), and is a staff reporter for *Business First*. Shook attended Dartmouth College, and received a B.A. from Wheaton College.

INDEX